MARCO  POLO

Travel with
**Insider
Tips**

CAPE TOWN

WINE LANDS, GARDEN ROUTE

ANGOLA   ZAMBIA

NAMIBIA   ZIMBABWE

BOTSWANA

Pretoria   ZAM-

ATLANTIC
OCEAN

www.r.

The best Insider Tips → p. 4

INSIDER TIP

Best of ... → p. 6

Sightseeing → p. 26

Food & Drink → p. 54

SYMBOLS

INSIDER TIP   Insider Tip

★   Highlight

●●●●   Best of ...

☼   Scenic view

Responsible travel: fair
trade principles and the
environment respected

**PRICE CATEGORIES
HOTELS**

Expensive   over 1600 rand

Moderate   800–1600 rand

Budget   under 800 rand

The prices are for two people
in a double room including
breakfast

**PRICE CATEGORIES
RESTAURANTS**

Expensive   over 200 rand

Moderate   120–200 rand

Budget   under 120 rand

The prices are for a 3-course
meal without drinks

7740136

On the cover: Impressive view from Table Mountain's summit p.45 | A tandem flight over Camps Bay p.43

marco-polo.com

CONTENTS

Shopping → p. 64

Entertainment → p. 72

Where to stay → p. 80

Street atlas → p. 124

MAPS IN THE GUIDEBOOK

(126 A1) Page numbers and coordinates refer to the street atlas
(0) Site/address located off the map. Coordinates are also given for places that are not marked on the street atlas
(U A1) Refers to the maps of the Cape Peninsula and Stellenbosch inside the back cover

INSIDE BACK COVER: PULL-OUT MAP →

PULL-OUT MAP 🗺

(🗺 A–B 2–3) Refers to the removable pull-out map
(🗺 a–b 2–3) Refers to the additional inset maps on the pull-out map

The best MARCO POLO Insider Tips

Our top 15 Insider Tips

INSIDER TIP **Culinary course**
Learn to cook Cape Malay food with the *Bo-Kaap Cooking Experience*. Residents in the Malay quarter open their doors to teach you the secrets of how to make the best samoosas or curry in the relaxed atmosphere of their homes → **p. 38**

INSIDER TIP **Float like a bird**
Paraglide tandem-style from Lion's Head and get a bird's eye view of the mansions and villas of Camps Bay! Discover Cape Town's diversity and beauty from high above (photo right) → **p. 43**

INSIDER TIP **The other Cape Town**
Take a tour of the townships and experience first-hand the hospitality of the locals that live in the suburbs away from Table Mountain. Head to *Mzoli's Place* in Gugulethu on a Saturday afternoon where tourists party with residents while enjoying a delicious piece of meat and a pint or two of the local brew → **p. 57**

INSIDER TIP **Concert in the park**
The *Kirstenbosch Botanical Gardens* turns into a lively concert stage on Sundays in the summer. Performances range from the Cape Town Philharmonic Orchestra (photo above) to some of South Africa's best bands → **p. 42**

INSIDER TIP **Sheer beach bliss**
It is a bit of a hike through some indigenous fynbos terrain to get to Cape Town's stunning and isolated *Sandy Bay* – be warned this is the city's unofficial nudist beach! → **p. 45**

INSIDER TIP **Matters of the heart**
See the operating theatre at the *Heart of Cape Town Museum* where the celebrated surgeon, Prof. Chris Barnard performed the world's first successful heart transplant in 1967 → **p. 47**

INSIDER TIP **Music sets the scene**
Mercury Live and Lounge is the hot spot for Cape Town's increasingly popular indie music scene → **p. 78**

INSIDER TIP **Fishing village for foodies**
The *Bay Harbour Market* in Hout Bay is where Capetonians from all walks of life gather at the weekend to take in live music, enjoy a good wine and indulge in great seafood → p. 69

INSIDER TIP **Pool with a view**
The *Guesthouse Bergzicht's* pool is the ideal place to cool off – it has a stunning view of Table Mountain → p. 83

INSIDER TIP **Hunger buster**
Simple and authentic best defines the small corner café and deli, *Mimi's*, in Lower Main Road in the student district of Observatory. Enjoy some delicious quiche as you people watch → p. 92

INSIDER TIP **Surfing for beginners**
Muizenberg is the best place to learn to surf in Cape Town. Enquire at one of the surf shops on the beach that hire out boards and wetsuits → p. 50

INSIDER TIP **Perfect pit stop**
Not to be missed on the Garden Route is a culinary feast at the Knysna forest *Phantom Forest* nature reserve – with stunning views across the lagoon → p. 101

INSIDER TIP **Say Cheese!**
Choose a spot in the sun at the *Fairview* wine estate and treat yourself to one of their gourmet cheese platters. Then stock up in their deli for the trip back to Cape Town before you leave → p. 108

INSIDER TIP **Gold leaf takes the cake**
High tea at the *Mount Nelson* luxury hotel surpasses all expectations – and the good news is that you don't have to be a resident to enjoy the sumptuous spread → p. 57

INSIDER TIP **Art in the making**
Galleries and the art scene have taken over the suburb of Woodstock in recent years. The best example of this trend is the *Bell-Roberts Contemporary Art Gallery* → p. 68

BEST OF ...

FOR FREE

● *Tantalise your taste buds*

On a Saturday many of the food stalls at the *Neighbourgoods Market* in Woodstock offer free samples. The tasty cheeses, biltong, tarts and pies are tempting enough to make you want to buy but there is no obligation to do so → p. 70

● *Kitesurfing spectacle*

Head to the *beach at Bloubergstrand* between December and March where some of the world's most talented kitesurfers offer spectators an amazing spectacle daily – free of charge! Go on a windy day and remember to take your camera (photo) → p. 48

● *Literature lovers*

Attend a reading by one of South Africa's leading authors on a Wednesday afternoon at the *Book Lounge* in the city centre, entrance is free of charge and they usually also provide a free glass of wine → p. 66

● *Art galore*

Cape Town is an artists' playground and their *galleries* – often part of their homes – are open to the public. Let the gallery attendants talk you through the art works. The best area for this is Lower Main Road in Observatory → p. 92

● *Beach volleyball*

Why pay to join a fitness studio during your stay when you can get a good workout on the beach? In *Camps Bay* someone always puts up volleyball nets on the beach at the weekend. Simply turn up and ask nicely if you can join in. A great way to make new friends! → p. 42

● *Tidal pools*

The sea water in Cape Town can be chilly and the waves intimidating but this need not put a damper on your holiday. You can still enjoy some fabulous swimming in tidal pools along the coast between *St James, Kalk Bay* and *Simon's Town*. The sun warms them up beautifully! → p. 50

● *Go up Table Mountain*

Postcard perfect and towering majestically above Cape Town is the much-photographed *Table Mountain* which draws its visitors like a magnet. The fit can hike up but the more obvious choice is to take the cable car. Either way the view from the top, over the city and the sea, is quite breathtaking → p. 45

● *Wine estates*

The *Constantia Wine Route* includes a number of famous wine estates. The oldest, *Groot Constantia*, goes back to the 17th century. The owners are doing an excellent job in retaining its historic feel while introducing a modern atmosphere with wine tastings, good restaurants and concerts → p. 42

● *Nelson Mandela's prison*

Former president Nelson Mandela spent 18 of the 27 years of his incarceration on the former prison island of *Robben Island*. Today the 'Sikhululekile' ferry takes visitors across from the V&A Waterfront – and the tours are conducted by ex-convicts → p. 40

● *Harbour entertainment hub*

You will be spoilt for choice at the *Victoria & Alfred Waterfront* shopping and entertainment precinct. Give yourself plenty of time to take in the harbour life with its variety of buskers, dance groups, restaurants, cinemas and so much more (photo) → p. 41

● *Sundowners by the sea*

Cape Town is known for having some of the world's most captivating sunsets. Capetonians celebrate this time of day with sundowners. Join in with a classic cocktail, a well chilled local beer or a Savanna cider. A good spot is at *Café Caprice* right by the beach in trendy Camps Bay → p. 41

● *Street party*

During the World Cup Soccer in 2010 tens of thousands of fans regularly came out to celebrate on the fan mile. No other street in Cape Town boasts as many restaurants, shops, street vendors and clubs as *Long Street*. The place rocks on a hot summer's night → p. 30

ONLY IN

BEST OF ...

AND IF IT RAINS?
Activities to brighten your day

● **Indoor golf**
Golfing pros may turn up their noses at *Cave Golf* in the V & A Waterfront but this mini golf course is a fun alternative when it rains. The 18-hole course makes for the perfect distraction for the entire family should the sun happen to take the day off → p. 94

● **Wine tasting**
Wine tasting is always popular, whatever the weather. At golfing great Ernie Els' wine estate you get to try seven of his finest wines. Once the clouds lift, you can sit out on the terrace and enjoy the superb views across the wine lands → p. 110

● **Rock climbing**
Why not use a rainy day for a climbing excursion? The *CityROCK Indoor Climbing Centre* has a climbing area of 4300ft² making it the country's largest climbing facility → p. 46

● **Perfectly dry underwater**
If some rainy days in August are starting to get to you, then why not visit the *Two Oceans Aquarium*. Enjoy this fascinating underwater world (photo) without the worry of getting wet → p. 41

● **Locker rooms that tell a tale**
Join a *Green Point Stadium* tour and take a peak behind the scenes and into the locker rooms. It was here that the teams would wait to meeting their opponents in the deciding matches in the Soccer World Cup 2010 → p. 93

● **Café society**
It's raining, it's pouring – but don't despair just take refuge in one of Cape Town's many inviting coffee shops. *Sidewalk Café* in Vredehoek comes highly recommend. Relax and enjoy! → p. 57

RAIN

RELAX AND CHILL OUT
Take it easy and spoil yourself

● *Historical baths*
Enter the distinctive blue *Long Street Baths* building and it feels as though you have stepped back in time to the 19th century but the pool and steam rooms have been modernised and are a great way to relax – and the Long and Kloof Street restaurants are just a few steps away → **p. 121**

● *Calming candles*
The *Equinox Spa* is renowned for its Swedish massage. Try their popular natural soya candle wax massage and you will be amazed at the relaxing effect it can have on a tired body (photo) → **p. 50**

● *Relaxation sans children*
The *Mount Nelson Hotel's Librisa Spa* offers dozens of wellness options. An added bonus is that they offer a free supervised children's activity area so you can unwind in peace → **p. 84**

● *Tea treat*
The wonderful spa experience at *Winchester Mansions* in Sea Point comes with a welcome bonus. Afterwards you can order teas and food from a health menu to complement your treatments → **p. 83**

● *African relaxation techniques*
Authentic African massage is the speciality of the spa at the *Cape Grace Hotel* – a colourful setting creates the perfect ambiance → **p. 84**

● *Floatation tank*
Forget your aching bones and feel rejuvenated after a day out sightseeing by spending some time in a floatation tank at the *Cape Town Medi-Spa*. Gently float until your body and soul is fully has recovered → **p. 121**

● *Hands-on wellness*
Eslinah Magemgenene may have lost her sight but her hands tell another story entirely. Take time out to let this blind therapist give you the most energising massage ever! → **p. 50**

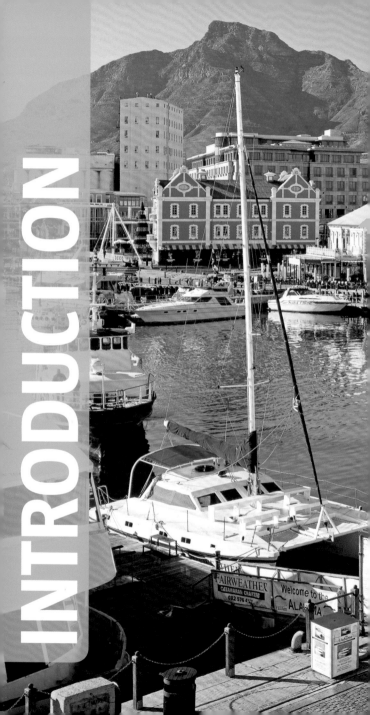

INTRODUCTION

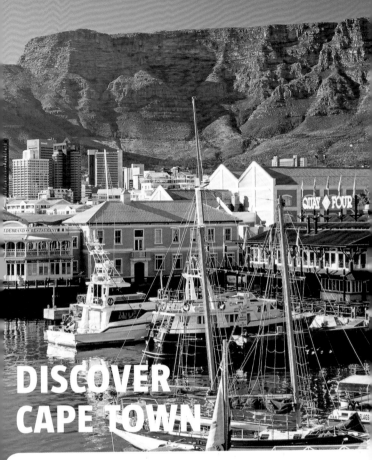

DISCOVER CAPE TOWN

A ritual takes place every year in Cape Town at Christmas time. On the first Sunday of Advent Capetonians flock to the four-laned Adderley Street which is closed to traffic for the afternoon. A stage is set up for the occasion and South Africa's pop stars and dancers entertain the crowds in anticipation of the big moment. As soon as it gets dark a switch is ceremoniously flipped and the city's colourful Christmas lights are switched on. As the countdown begins, the master of ceremony asks the crowd: 'Isn't Cape Town the most beautiful city in the world?' and tens of thousands of Capetonians raise their voices in agreement.

Moments like this make it clear just how proud the people of Cape Town are of their city. It is South Africa's oldest city and is know as the Mother City – the mother of all South African cities. More than 300 years ago the first European settlers set up camp here. They too would have probably been as captivated by the natural beauty of Table Mountain as any visitor today.

Photo: Victoria & Alfred Waterfront

At the focal point the metropolis (population of around three million) is 1086m/3563ft high Table Mountain in all its majestic glory. Nestled below in its shadow lies the city centre and business district where skyscrapers stand tall alongside small Victorian houses. Sprawling out on both sides of Table Mountain and flanked by several rocky mountain chains are numerous suburbs, all with very different atmospheres. From the chic and stylish Camps Bay on the one side to the student district of Observatory on the other. Only once you get to look down from Table Mountain across the vast expanse that stretches south towards the horizon do you get a feel for how big the city really is. Two million of its residents, i.e. two thirds of its population live away from the mountains and the sea in densely populated urban areas and low income townships. The peninsula – at the head of which lies Cape Town – stretches all the way to the Cape of Good Hope. Here the landscape is a mix of idyllic seaside villages and wild and seemingly untouched nature.

Table Mountain metropolis

What makes Cape Town and its surroundings so unique is the generous natural beauty that nature has bestowed on this southerly tip of Africa. The magnificent mountain range that spans the peninsula not only makes for excellent hiking trails but also allows you to see panoramic vistas that you would normally only get to see from an aircraft just as it is about to land. The clear Atlantic Ocean washes its chilly waters

Long Street is one of the liveliest and most popular streets in central Cape Town

onto sun kissed beaches, and there are so many beaches that everyone is guaranteed a spot in the soft sand and the sun. On the Atlantic side are places like Clifton and Camps Bay, where the in-crowd hangs out by day and then flaunts their new tans at the stylish cafés on the promenade in the evening. Across the way is False Bay where the warmer waters are more family-friendly and ideal for picnics and beach ball games. Above them all the hot summer sun rises at six in the morning and then dips into the ocean with spectacular sun sets in the evening.

The beauty Capetonians are surrounded by is infectious and seems to spill over into their nature and their friendliness is as well known and as unshakeable as Table Mountain itself. They are as proud

Township versus world class city

of their relaxed lifestyle as they are of the charm of the city. Some locals will tell you with a wry smile that the reason it is known as the Mother City is because everything takes at least nine months to get done! This relaxed and leisurely way of life is however in no way to blame for the enormous challenges still facing the city – almost a full two decades after the first democratic elections in 1994. The transition to democracy and the legacy of apartheid means that the city still faces an ongoing political and administrative tug of war leaving many key problems seemingly unsolvable. One of the biggest challenges is the fact that there is still a huge divide between the

wealthy minority and poor majority, who struggle with the consequences of their extreme poverty. The HIV/Aids pandemic, that has South Africa at its epicentre, predominantly affects the poor in the townships. When Nelson Mandela spoke to the cheering masses from the balcony of city hall in February 1990 after his release, it was the first step in the establishment of a new democracy. In reality however it will take a long time for Cape Town to become the rainbow nation that the country's flag optimistically symbolises. The city's various population groups still tend to keep very much to themselves. Cape Town's residents are made up of Afrikaners (whose ancestors were Dutch immigrants), the English-speaking community (descendent of British immigrants), the indigenous black community and the so-called 'coloured' community (descendent of Europeans and African and Asian slaves). Many residents were counting on the 2010 World Cup Soccer tournament to help solve the city's social problems and give it a new lease on life. However, the tournament did not bring with it the hoped for visitor numbers nor the job creation. In fact hundreds of thousands of jobs have been lost in response to the ongoing economic crisis that started in 2008 – mostly in the mining sector, the backbone of the South African economy. Unemployment mostly affects the country's young adolescents who regularly stage service delivery protests against the African National Congress (ANC) government.

To understand why so many different population groups live in the shadow of Table Mountain one has to back through Cape Town's 300-year history. The city's founders were Dutch seafarers who established a supply station, the *Vereenigde Oost Indische Compagnie (VOC)* here to supply produce for the trade they conducted between the Netherlands and Southeast Asia. In the 17th and 18th century, governors Jan van Riebeeck and Simon van der Stel turned the halfway station into a flourishing colony. However, its prosperity did not benefit everyone. The indigenous African population found itself subjugated to slavery, as did the workers imported from Southeast Asia. By the end of the 18th century the flagship of the Dutch shipping company sank, the VOC went bankrupt and the British took command of the colony. At this time Cape Town was a thriving provincial town even if it lacked status. When the world's biggest diamond rush began in Kimberley (halfway between Cape Town and Johannesburg) in the 19th century, and gold was later discovered in Johannesburg, Cape Town with its harbour developed into an important shipping hub. In 1910 Cape Town finally became the legislative capital of the Union of South Africa established by the British and to this day parliament sits in Cape Town and its legislative system is based on the one used by its British founders.

City with a poignant past

The apartheid era in the 20th century cemented the city's existing social structures. The Group Areas Act of 1950 was used to justify the forced removal of black and coloured communities from many of the city's prime areas. Today the city's white population continue to reside mainly in the well-to-do coastal areas or in the city's quiet and leafy suburbs. A large majority of the residents live outside of the centre in the city's sprawling informal shanty towns and low income townships. South Africa's social divide – one of the world's largest – is even more evident in Cape Town. A microcosm of the severity of the situation is Imizamo Yethu, a township a mere stone's throw from the chic homes of Hout Bay. Here 18,000 people live in an area designed in the early 1990s for only a fraction of that number. The housing problem has also been further exacerbated by the country's lax immigration policies that have seen millions of refugees, from countries like Zimbabwe and Mozambique, coming into South Africa and competing with the locals for low-wage jobs which add to the existing social tensions. The level of poverty is not as apparent in Cape Town now as it was in the past because the city deals with its beggars far more proactively than anywhere else in the country.

A number of white South Africans seem to have the tendency to be pessimistic about the country's future. However even though the country is plagued by corruption, the fact of the matter is that the situation for whites is by comparison still better than for other South Africans. Over 70 per cent of executive positions are in white hands and even the lower middle class white

A challenging time ahead

families can afford to have a servant in the home. The social divide between rich and poor is even more apparent today than at the end of the apartheid era. Key to reversing this is education. South Africa spends seven per cent of its gross domestic product on education, more than any other African country. Sadly this outlay is not delivering tangible results. South Africa's ideal rainbow nation as envisaged by former Archbishop Desmond Tutu will still be in the making for a long time yet.

One question that anyone travelling to Cape Town will no doubt ask, is whether or not the city is safe for tourists. If you abide by the usual unwritten safety rules there

The breath-taking view from Table Mountain over Lion's Head and the city

is no reason why you cannot experience this metropolis as a city that is as safe as it is beautiful. Keep in mind this guiding principle: undue anxiety is as debilitating as downright carelessness *(see the section titled 'Rather safe than sorry', p. 37)*. This way you can look forward to a city whose amazing beauty will captivate you as much as the spirit of its people. And when you look out of your aeroplane window for your final glimpse of the city and Table Mountain you will understand just why Capetonians are so proud of their home.

WHAT'S HOT

1 Let's dance

Zumba Its samba and salsa rhythms will have you work up a sweat in no time. This dance workout is catching on fast in Cape Town. Let Abigail Kwan take you through the steps at *Take Down (89 Main Road, Diep River)* or at the *Jion Martial Arts and Fitness Centre (Corner Main Rd/Summerley Rd)*. The *Virgin Active Health Club (21 Lower Long St, www.virginactive. co.za)* also offers visitors programmes to burn off the holiday excesses. And, if you are thinking of hosting your own Zumba party look no further than *Zumba Fitness (www.zumba-fitness.co.za)*.

Midnight snack 2

Picnic Full moon picnics are the latest Cape Town trend and the place is Lion's Head. Hike your way to the top equipped with a blanket and picnic. For a fully organised full moon picnic on Paarl Mountain contact the *Taal Museum* – you can even pre-order a hamper *(www. taalmuseum.co.za, photo)*. Other options are the full moon hike up Klapmutskop in Stellenbosch with the *Dirtopia Trail Centre*, starting with sundowners and a picnic overlooking Table Mountain *(R 44, Delvera Farm Stellenbosch, www.dirtopia.co.za)*.

3 Volunteer tourism

Captivating Outings like whale watching and shark cage diving attract visitors to Cape Town's coast all year round, but how about joining *Voluntours (www.voluntours.co.za, photo)*, a volunteer tourism organisation that helps stranded sea mammals, among other activities? Extra hands are always welcome. Still need a souvenir or two? Then try trendy *Monkey Biz (43 Rose St, www.monkeybiz.co.za)* in the knowledge that you are supporting township residents. Even by booking your accommodation through *www.fairtourismsa.org.za* garners your support for a worthwhile cause.

On the catwalk

Cape fashion Urban African best describes the fashionable creations by Stefania Morland. This South African clothing designer relies on sensual cuts, luxurious materials and easy-to-wear designs *(corner Orange St/ Gray's Pass, stefaniamorland.com)*. Ilan is the label for you if you are on the look-out for en eye-catching outfit. Designer Stephan Martin is well known for his evening gowns but he also designs casual wear – with the emphasis on sustainable fashion *(at Bromwell, 250 Albert Road, photo)*. *Sitting Pretty* has its roots in Thailand and Cape Town and the designs bear testimony to these sources of inspiration. Well worth a visit, this boutique also sells other sought after local labels *(111 Long St)*.

Taking Woodstock

The place to be Woodstock is definitely Cape Town's up-and-coming art district. An old industrial area full of factories and warehouses that now house galleries or restaurants like the *Woodstock Lounge & Bar*. Here you can enjoy some live music, daring cocktails and excellent bar food *(70 Roodebloem Rd)* while the truly trendy satisfy their hunger pangs at *The Test Kitchen*, where – contrary to its name – the dishes served are all tried and tested. The owner and head chef is none other than South African celebrity chef Luke Dale-Roberts *(The Old Biscuit Mill, 375 Albert Rd, photo)*. The *Old Biscuit Mill* is definitely worth a visit for its melange of restaurants and delis, bakeries and cute shops and art galleries. For some excellent artworks try *Greatmore Studios (47–49 Greatmore St, www.great moreart.org)*.

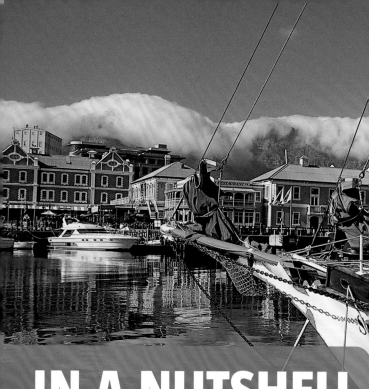

IN A NUTSHELL

BABOONS

Wild baboons live all over the peninsula and they are a popular draw card for visitors to the Cape of Good Hope where they are most prevalent. On the road out to the reserve and in the reserve itself you will stand a good chance of encountering a troop. But be warned! They can be quite assertive, even dangerous and the cheekiest among them will rob you of your picnic if they can see or smell it.

BILTONG

If a *braai* is not on the cards then there is always biltong. For the uninitiated biltong is strips of air dried meat (similar to American beef jerky) and it is South Africa's most beloved snack, eaten any time be it at a sports event, or at work or in the pub. You can buy it just about anywhere, and there are even shops that specialise in biltong that have large pieces of it on their walls, waiting to be sliced. Biltong has its cultural heritage in the Boer pioneers centuries ago. They would cure their meat with vinegar, salt and coriander and then air dry it in the sun to preserve it for their treks through the African bush. Today the production process is far more hygienic. The trekkers used to place raw meat under their horse's saddle – the motion tenderised the meat and the perspiration salted it.

Photo: The V&A Waterfront

From greedy baboons to the Cape Doctor: all there is to know – quirky or otherwise – about this metropolis on the Cape peninsula

BRAAI

Braai is the Afrikaans word meaning 'to grill' – and this social gathering is a favourite pastime for Capetonians. Steak, ribs, filet, ostrich steaks, boerewors (the local sausage), all kinds of vegetables, fish and crayfish: they all land up on the *braai* grid. One of the phrases you will hear most often in Cape Town is: 'You must come round for a braai!'

CAPE DOCTOR

In the summer months – from December to March – the south easter, a strong trade wind, sometimes makes itself felt on the peninsula. It blows through the city taking the smog with it which is why it is known locally as the Cape Doctor, and it is also responsible for the famous tablecloth of clouds that occasionally adorns Table Mountain. If its blows for a

The District Six Museum documents the history of the razed suburb

few days in a row, it rattles the nerves of the locals.

CAR GUARDS

Car guards in their distinctive yellow vests represent the poorest South Africans, the lowest income sector. Tens of thousands of them direct cars into parking spaces around South Africa every day and promise to keep an eye on your car. They usually do the promised job and some bona fide ones are officially registered with the city authorities. A tip of at least five rand is the going rate.

COLOURED COMMUNITY

While black people make up about three quarters of South Africa's population, making them the largest population group, these ratios are very different in the Cape. Here the coloured community is dominant making up 50 per cent of the population. Whites and blacks make up the remaining 50 per cent, both almost equally. The coloured community is partly descendant from relationships between white colonists and indigenous Khoisan and descendant from Muslim slaves from Asia, the Cape Malay. During the apartheid years people who were neither unequivocally white nor black in appearance, were classified as coloured. At the time many families were torn apart because various members were classified according to different population groups.

DISA PARK TOWERS

The three Disa Park Towers are loathed by Capetonians for defacing the otherwise pristine view of Devil's Peak alongside Table Mountain. The city fathers, determined to protect the view of the majestic mountain, imposed stringent building height restrictions. In the 1960s the Disa Park Towers developer discovered a loophole in the law that allowed the notorious building to be built in the suburb of Vredehoek – just outside the limits of the building restriction zone. The developers were undeterred and they managed to destroy the panoramic view others had tried so hard to uphold. The only people in support of the Disa Park Towers today are its residents who are afforded an amazing view. The towers have since earned themselves some very derisory nicknames.

DISTRICT SIX

Cape Town's major scar from the apartheid era is *District Six* – a fallow wasteland in the middle of the city. In the 1960s 60,000 residents of this once lively quarter were forcibly relocated to townships under the Group Area Act – a government decree that determined the segregation of races into demarcated regions. On 11 February 1966 District Six was declared an exclusively white suburb. The multicultural suburb was ostensibly too close for comfort to the city centre for the authorities. The official reason given for the removal of its residents was that this was the only way to get the upper hand on crime. All the homes were torn down and all that remains of the suburb are a few churches and mosques that remained unscathed. The suburb was renamed 'Zonnebloem' (sunflower) but even giving it an attractive new name did not change the fact that nobody wanted to build there any longer. Even the white people were against the destruction of the suburb at the time. In the interim the first of the displaced people have begun returning with their families. The landownership, reallocation and rebuilding process is mired in red tape and the reconstruction process will no doubt take a very long time.

HOWZIT?

Take the time to experience the country to the full even if it means just taking a few moments to engage in some social pleasantries. You can expect to hear 'Howzit?' everywhere; it is a South African slang derivative of 'How is it going?' and it is very popular with the youth. Only once the niceties are out of the way can you get down to the matter at hand.

KAAPSTAD

This is the Afrikaans word for Cape Town and you will see it on road signs heading into the city. Afrikaans is a language with its roots in Dutch and was the language of the apartheid regime. Today it is one of South Africa's eleven official languages alongside English and key African languages like Xhosa and Zulu.

MINIBUS TAXIS

You will hear them hooting frantically on all the main roads but don't be alarmed! These small 16-seater buses are simply trying to attract potential commuters by letting them know that they are available. It is, however, a good idea to keep your distance from them when driving. One minute they will be driving for their lives, the next minute they slam on breaks right in front of you. Although it may seem chaotic they do have set routes and are well organised. Commuters use different hand signals to indicate the destination they are after. The driver stops abruptly anywhere on the road and the passenger climbs in. It is the most authentic mode of transport in Cape Town, but a word of caution: they do have a very high accident rate – only use them during the day and only if you really have to.

RADIO

Radio is still the most influential medium in many parts of Africa. South Africa is no exception and it has some excellent stations to help you while away the time on long road trips. *Five FM* has the country's best DJs. You get a good idea of the mood in the country and social topics on *567 CapeTalk*, the sister station to Johannesburg's *Talk Radio 702*. Most of the stations can also be picked up via live streaming on the Internet, which means you can still get a feel of South Africa in your everyday life back home.

SANGOMAS

The belief in supernatural powers is something non-African cultures view with a certain amount of skepticism. This is hardly fair when you consider how many other nations are superstitious about Friday the thirteenth or fear a black cat crossing their path or walking under ladders. Having said that, South Africa does take this issue to another level with more than 200,000 *sangomas* or traditional healers, hardly a negligible figure. These *sangomas* earn their money by making contact with the ancestors for a diagnosis. Many South Africans have taken recourse, at least once, to the controversial healing services provided by *sangomas*. In all fairness, many of them are healers in their own right basing their profession on the medicinal value of herbs, roots and other indigenous plants.

SHANGAAN ELECTRO

It is almost impossible to be a party-pooper in South Africa: people dance in the townships, at clubs, in the stadiums and in bars. Even Jacob Zuma, who was in charge of the prison choir when he was a political prisoner on Robben Island, never let an election campaign go by (ahead of his accession to presidency in April 2009) without laying on a dance performance. At present Shangaan Electro new wave dance music is filtering into Cape Town from the dance clubs of Soweto. It has a ridiculously high tempo, impossibly fast beats, is laden with marimba sounds and has its origins in traditional afro-dance music. To experience it first-hand you have to hit the Cape Town clubs.

SHEBEENS

The shebeen has its origins in the Irish word *sibín* = little jug. The origin is disputed as many believe it to be derived from the Zulu word *shibhile* which means cheap. Either way, in South Africa shebeens refer to the illegal bars in the township that were run without a license during the apartheid era and where home brew was served. Most of them are now operated legally but the name shebeen remains alive and well. Some are well worth a visit but be sure to have a good tour guide accompany you!

SPORT

During his 27 years as a political prisoner Nelson Mandela got up every morning at 4.30am and jogged on the spot in his cell, much to the chagrin of his fellow inmates and he continued to jog regularly when he became president of South Africa. Sport is also integral to the everyday life of many Capetonians so why not join them on the Sea Point promenade. It is the ideal place to go for an early morning jog with the 2010 World Cup Soccer Stadium on the one side and the Atlantic Ocean on the other. Here the waves break right up against the promenade. Spectator sports are also hugely popular so if soccer is your thing then you can spur on Bafana Bafana – the boys – or if it is rugby then the Springboks are the nation's international success story. Buy yourself the distinctive green jersey and do as South Africans do: hang out at one of the rugby pubs to cheer along their team. Everybody gets very emotional! During the Rugby World Cup held in South Africa in 1995 and 2007 the streets were completely empty with everyone glued to their television sets.

VUVUZELAS

You either love them or hate them! Be that as it may, ever since the 2010 World Cup Soccer in South Africa everyone knows the distinctive noisy sound these long plastic trumpets make. Nobody really knows who started them and their origins are still being fought over. A fan of one of the Johannesburg soccer clubs, Kaizer Chiefs, alleges that he invented the instrument making it from a bicycle hooter. The African Shembe church says it has been around for ages in the form of kudu horns. Today the debate continues, as does the cacophony of sound it produces ahead of any big match.

No soccer match is complete without the vuvuzela

THE PERFECT DAY
Cape Town in 24 hours

07:00am HOP ON HOP OFF

If you only have 24 hours in Cape Town you need to make the best of it so don't waste any time hiring a car. What you should rather do is head straight for the *Citysightseeing Cape Town Hop On – Hop Off bus* (bus stops and bookings at *www.citysightseeing.co.za, tel. 021 5 11 60 00;* tickets also sold on the bus). The distinctive open-top red double decker bus leaves every 15 minutes. The 'Blue Mini Peninsula Tour' covers the city's main attractions. Headphones provide you with a guided tour – in 16 languages. Hop off at the stops that interest you and simply wait for the next bus when you are ready to hop on again. Start your tour at whatever bus stop you prefer.

08:00am THE CITY COMES TO LIFE

It's not a good idea to skip breakfast on a sightseeing-filled day! Don't worry, you won't miss the bus, the *Hop On – Hop Off* only gets going from 9am onwards with the exception of a direct route to Table Mountain. If you are starting your tour from the city centre then the cafés near *Long Street → p. 30* (photo left) are a good option. Early mornings in Cape Town, when the natural lighting is at its best, are excellent photo opportunities and there is no shortage of subject matter. Your first bus stop is within easy reach outside Cape Town Tourism's Burg Street Information Centre.

09:15am A WALK IN THE PARK

Take the bus out of the buzzing city centre and enjoy the ride through the leafy suburbs and hop off at Kirstenbosch, Cape Town's world renowned *Botanical Gardens → p. 42*. Spend an hour absorbing its beauty and imbibing the natural earth energy of *Table Mountain → p. 45* and then you will be bursting with engery and ready to resume your day.

10:30am FOOD & WINE

Hop on to the next bus which will only take you one stop further to the Constantia Nek Wine Tour interchange. Get off here and hop on to the *Free Wine Tour* to *Groot Constantia → p. 42* (photo right), South Africa's oldest wine estate. Indulge in some wine tasting and have lunch at the excellent *Jonkershuis Restaurant*.

Get to know some of the most dazzling, exciting and relaxing facets of Cape Town — all in a single day

02:00pm TOWNSHIP TOUR

Once the bus has brought you back to the Constantia Nek interchange, hop back on to the 'Blue Mini Peninsula Tour'. Hop off at the *Imizamo Yethu Township* bus stop. It is important to check with the tourist office which *township tours* → p. 46 leave from there and how long they take. Only those who have seen how the other half live, will have a full picture of the reality of everyday life in Cape Town. The hospitality of the people living here is often quite heartwarming.

05:00pm BEACH CAFÉS

From one extreme to another: once back on the bus your next stop is *Camps Bay* → p. 41 (photo). The pristine beach is only a half an hour drive away. Choose one of the many street cafés along the beach. Only once you sit down to a leisurely cappuccino does the social dichotomy that is Cape Town truly hits home. The stark contrast between the haves and the have-nots is an everyday reality in South Africa and will leave you with a lasting impression.

07:30pm AS THE EVENING WEARS ON

Your last stop to hop off at is the *Victoria & Alfred Waterfront* → p. 41. Enjoy sunset beside the water's edge with a sumptuous seafood platter or a delicious steak at the *Harbour House*, a trendy new restaurant next to the amphitheatre. You could of course spend the rest of the evening in the huge shopping and entertainment emporium but an even better option is to take a taxi to 273 *Long Street* and go to the *Waiting Room* → p. 78, one of Cape Town's most sought after clubs. Enjoy a Savannah — a dry local cider — while you recap the events of your day or dance the night away with Cape Town's top DJs, who perform here every night.

Citysightseeing Cape Town Bus
Suggested starting point: Tourism Centre Burg Street
Adults 140 rand, children 70 rand

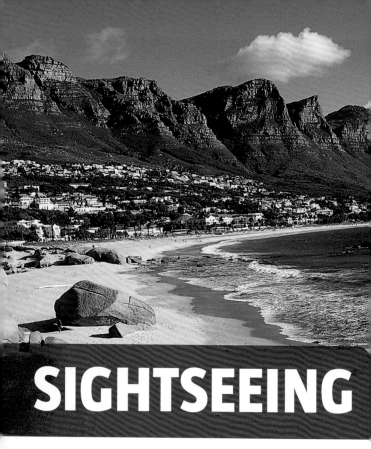

SIGHTSEEING

CITY **WHERE TO START?**
Signal Hill (128 B3) *(𝄢 E3)*:
there is hardly any other metropolis
in the world that is dominated by a
mountain backdrop in the way that
Cape Town is. The quickest way to
get your bearings is to take a drive
up Signal Hill which will give you an
excellent view across the city. The
view may not be as good as from
Lion's Head but it is easily reached
by car and there is ample parking at
the top. Also a favourite picnic spot
for Capetonians.

One could say that Cape Town – with Table
Mountain, the ocean and its historical
sites – has more than its fair share of attractions for one city. Cape Town is indeed
a city with a rich history, as evidenced by
its many museums, but it also has beautiful white beaches that go on forever.
You get the best overview of the city from
Table Mountain. The view from its summit
is breath-taking and you should really put
aside at least half a day for an outing. It
will also give you a good idea of the sites
you will want to explore later on. Once
you get back down, the decision of where
to head to first can be quite overwhelming. To the beach? Or to one of the cafés

Photo: Camps Bay with the Twelve Apostles in the background

Between mountains and sea: for a true idea of Cape Town take a stroll through its fascinating history and along its pristine beaches

in the trendy urban areas like the Cape Quarter or Long Street? Or how about taking in some cultural history?

The museums that come highly recommended are those that give you an insight into the history of the city. The *District Six Museum* and the *Jewish Museum* give you some insights into life in the Cape. Entrance fees are generally reasonable, usually around 30 rand (approx. 2.70 euros). Art lovers in particular will get good value for their money if they are interested in art works from the colonial times. Various museums, like the *Castle of Good Hope*, not only display art from this period but also have exhibits that showcase aspects of how life was lived in the Cape in the past. You will also find some of the works of Dutch and Flemish masters in Cape Town. However, those interested in con-

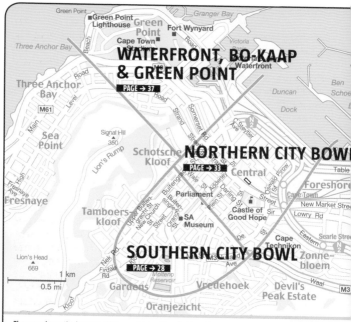

The map shows the location of the most interesting districts. There is a detailed map of each district on which each of the sights described is numbered.

temporary and modern art have a more limited choice. The only venue is the *South African National Gallery*. The permanent display may be modest but there are always temporary exhibitions of interesting South African artists that make a visit to the gallery worthwhile. To get a good idea of the local art scene, it is definitely worth popping into the city's private galleries.

You should also visit one of the city's townships – after all half of Cape Town's population lives in townships. There are many tour operators who organise private tours. Instead of looking down at the roofs of the shacks from your air-conditioned bus, you are taken around by locals and get to talk to them first-hand.

SOUTHERN CITY BOWL

The hollow beneath Table Mountain, flanked on the one side by the Signal Hill range and on the other by Devil's Peak, is known locally as the City Bowl.

The City Bowl is made up of suburbs like Gardens, Oranjezicht, Tamboerskloof and Vredehoek. Residential areas characterised by quaint Victorian houses, many of which are guest houses, restaurants and shops. While the area facing Table Mountain has central Long Street (the party mile), the leafy Company's Gardens, the adjoining Houses of Parliament and several interesting museums. When the shops close at five in the evening the office workers rush home and the city centre completely shuts down, with the exception of Long Street and a few surrounding streets. For years the private sector, together with city planners, has been looking into initiatives involving millions of rands in investments aimed at giving the city a new lease on life.

🔳 CAPE TOWN HOLOCAUST CENTRE/ SOUTH AFRICAN JEWISH MUSEUM
(129 D5–6) (*∅ G5*)

For a century and a half Jewish immigrants and their descendents have played an integral part in South Africa's culture, economy and politics. The *South African Jewish Museum* gives the visitor an impressive insight into this community's role in the country's history. Partly housed in one of the country's first synagogues, dating back to 1863, the exhibit includes video footage of witnesses who talk of their struggle, alongside the ANC, against the apartheid government. Across from the museum is the *Cape Town Holocaust Centre* where you will get a poignant insight into the crimes against humanity committed during World War Two – visual and audio footage. Don't forget to bring your passport which you have to present to security at the entrance. *Sun–Thu 10am–5pm, Fri 10am–2pm | www. sajewishmuseum.co.za | 88 Hatfield Street | Central*

🔳 COMPANY'S GARDENS ⭐
(129 D5) (*∅ G5*)

Situated in the heart of the city, the Gardens is a shady oasis popular with strolling tourists and Capetonians enjoy their lunch breaks on its benches and lawns. Tucked away under the shade of the magnificent trees is an outdoor café serving light meals *(Gardens Tea Room | daily 7am–7pm | tel. 021 4 23 29 19)*. *Government Avenue*, Cape Town's museum mile – flanked by mighty

---

⭐ **Company's Gardens**
Museum mile and a leafy city centre oasis → p. 29

⭐ **Castle of Good Hope**
Imposing fort that is a testimony to the first settlers in the Cape → p 33

⭐ **District Six Museum**
A fitting tribute to a suburb with a tragic past → p. 34

⭐ **Bo-Kaap**
Colourful houses and mosques nestled below Signal Hill → p. 38

⭐ **De Waterkant**
Alleyways, boutiques, restaurants and wine bars → p. 38

⭐ **Robben Island**
Nelson Mandela's prison for almost 20 years → p. 40

⭐ **Table Mountain**
Iconic landmark with panoramic views → p. 45

⭐ **Groot Constantia**
South Africa's oldest wine estate in a stunning setting → p. 42

⭐ **Victoria & Alfred Waterfront**
Entertainment and shopping precinct in the harbour → p. 41

⭐ **Kirstenbosch National Botanical Gardens**
Magnificent setting and more than 7000 plant species → p. 42

⭐ **Cape of Good Hope**
The picturesque Cape Point headland is well worth a visit → p. 51

MARCO POLO HIGHLIGHTS

old oak trees – runs alongside the park. The Company's Gardens takes its name from the Dutch East India Company that set it up as a vegetable garden. The British statesman and diamond magnate, Cecil John Rhodes had a statue erected here in his own honour. And the squirrels that scurry around the park are also his legacy – it was he who introduced them to the Cape. *Between Orange St and Wale St | Central*

Neoclassical Victorian – the Houses of Parliament

■3 HOUSES OF PARLIAMENT
(129 D5) (Ⓜ G5)

The city's parliament buildings are steeped in history. It was here that many of the laws and policies that defined the apartheid were passed. Hendrik Verwoerd, the architect of apartheid, was assassinated here. Assassin Dimitri Tsafendas later claimed that a tapeworm he harboured had instructed him to commit the murder. A tour through the passages of the Houses of Parliament gives the visitor further insights into just how apartheid manifested itself: the building was designed in such a way that each racial group was forced to remain separate from the other. Bear in mind that parliament only convenes here a few months a year and the chances of getting a glimpse of today's president are very slim. The president, who is not a member of parliament, is rarely in Cape Town. To join a guided tour you need to book a week in advance and don't forget to take your passport. *Mon–Fri 9am, 10am, 11am, noon | tel. 021 4 03 33 41 | www.parliament.gov.za | Parliament St | Central*

■4 KLOOF STREET
(128 B–C 5–6) (Ⓜ E6–F5)

The area around Kloof Street and its side streets is the hub of the city's creative scene. It is here that e.tv, one of the nationwide television broadcasters, has its headquarters and where Capetonians spend entire afternoons on their laptops in its many cafés. Take the opportunity to explore the city's rich sub-culture and browse through some of the street's many trendy boutiques, shops and record stores like *Mabu Vinyl (Rheede Centre | 2 Rheede Street)*.

■5 LONG STREET ●
(129 D5–E3) (Ⓜ F5–G4)

Long Street is where Capetonians from all walks of life come together, it is a part

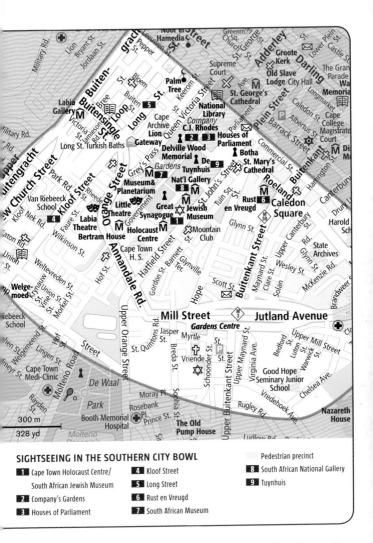

SIGHTSEEING IN THE SOUTHERN CITY BOWL

1 Cape Town Holocaust Centre/
   South African Jewish Museum
2 Company's Gardens
3 Houses of Parliament
4 Kloof Street
5 Long Street
6 Rust en Vreugd
7 South African Museum
8 South African National Gallery
9 Tuynhuis

Pedestrian precinct

of the city that never sleeps and it is a great place to spend the day. The charming street cafés are perfect for an afternoon of people watching. At night the in-crowd makes its way from one bar to the next. Long Street is a colourful and eclectic mix of fast food restaurants and stylish bou-tique hotels, shops selling African crafts and small hip-hop bars with dance floors are not much bigger than a ping-pong table. Many of the houses are typically Victorian and their balconies jut out over the pavements. The balconies are sup-ported by filigreed columns turning the pavements into romantic arcades. Besides numerous cafés, restaurants and clubs, Long Street also has trendy boutiques with clothes by South African and international designers, as well as some of the city's most interesting art galleries.

Traditional dance costume in the South African Museum

6 RUST EN VREUGD
(129 D5) *(ɯ G5)*

This building which dates back to 1778, was declared a listed building in 1940 and is one of the best examples of 18th century Cape architecture. The façade was designed by German sculptor Anton Anreith. The exhibits form part of the *William Fehr Collection*, the greater part of which is on display at the Castle of Good Hope. They are from the 16th and 19th century and document people and events at the Cape.

The garden was restored in the mid 1980s using 18th century designs. *Tue–Thu 10am–5pm | www.iziko.org.za/rustvreugd | 78 Buitenkant St | Central*

7 SOUTH AFRICAN MUSEUM
(129 D5) *(ɯ F–G5)*

This is the oldest museum in southern Africa and dates back to 1825. It documents the subcontinent's nature and culture in great detail and even has an exhibit that is a reconstructed cave with rock art. There is a large fossil collection and you get to see the 20m/65ft long skeleton of a blue whale. The city's planetarium adjoins it. *Daily 10am–5pm | www.iziko.org.za/sam | 25 Queen Victoria St | Central*

8 SOUTH AFRICAN NATIONAL GALLERY (129 D5) *(ɯ F–G5)*

The museum is one of the most famous in the country and houses a vast collection of European and African art from the last few centuries, as well as regular temporary exhibitions of contemporary art. *Tue–Sun 10am–5pm | www.iziko.org.za/sang | Government Ave | Central*

9 TUYNHUIS
(129 D5) *(ɯ G5)*

From the Company's Gardens you can get a good view of Tuynhuis, which was built in 1700 as accommodation for officials from the Dutch East India Company or *Vereenigden Oost-Indischen Compagnie (VOC)*. It was modified and rebuilt numerous times over the centuries. Its triangular gable, depicting the VOC banner held by two figures from Greek mythology, is attributed to Anton Anreith who was also responsible for a number of other city facades. Today Tuynhuis is where the state president receives dignitaries on state visits. Capetonians tell stories of how Nelson Mandela, during his term in office, would often walk through the Tynhuis garden and chat to astonished tourists through the slats of the fence. *As a rule can only be viewed from outside. For tours inside enquire at the tourist office | Government Ave | Central*

NORTHERN CITY BOWL

It is mainly high-rise office blocks – whose lights illuminate the entire inner city at night – that characterise the lower or northern part of the City Bowl. This area is also where you will find many historical buildings that are reminiscent of the time when Cape Town was a trading post between Europe and Southeast Asia and later becoming an apartheid stronghold. It is also where you will find the famous St George's Cathedral, which was the seat of the Anglican Archbishop Desmond Tutu's brave and relentless struggle against the apartheid system.

■1 CASTLE OF GOOD HOPE ★
(129 E–F5) *(𝄢 H5)*

This landmark star shaped fortress is located right in the middle of town. It is South Africa's oldest colonial building and was designed on European models and built by the Dutch East India Company (VOC) between 1666 and 1679. On the free tours through the compound you also get to see the castle dungeons. There is a blacksmith's forge and various museums. The very impressive *William Fehr Collection* includes paintings, furniture and everyday items dating from the beginnings of colonial South Africa until the mid 19th century. Representations of everyday life in Cape Town give the visitor a real insight into what it must have been like to live in colonial times, and the role

that both European and Asian influences played. The *Castle Military Museum* gives an overview of Cape Town's military history. *Daily 9.30am–4pm, tours are free of charge Mon–Fri 11am, noon and 2pm | tel. 021 7 87 10 89 | www.castleofgoodhope. co.za | corner Buitenkant St/Darling St | Central*

■2 CITY HALL/GRAND PARADE
(129 E5) *(𝄢 H5)*

Built in 1905 in the Italian Renaissance style, it was (until recently) home to the offices of the city of Cape Town and the city library. Its tower is a replica of London's

LOW BUDGET

▶ *Cape Town Partnership* – an organisation whose aim it is to advance the development of Cape Town's city centre – offers a variety of free city tours. One will take you through the eastern part of the city centre so you can familiarise yourself with the *city hall* and the *Grand Parade.* There is also a special tour that gives you insights into new building and investment projects in the city centre. Keen to know more about Cape Town's shopping hot spots? Then join a shopping tour of the city's markets and boutiques *(tel. 021 4 91 18 81 | www.capetown partnership.co.za).*

▶ The climb up *Lion's Head* can be daunting at the best of times, so why not join *Friends of Lion's Head?* They often take groups up this landmark on unusual routes for a small donation. *www.friendsoflionshead. org.za*

Big Ben. It was on the city hall balcony that Nelson Mandela made his first public appearance in February 1990 immediately after his release from captivity in the Paarl wine lands. More than 100,000 jubilant supporters waited for hours on the *Grand Parade* – today this square in front of city hall is used as a car park and market. Concerts are still held in the city hall auditorium. *Interior can only be viewed when a concert is on (see 'Entertainment') | Dale St | Central*

■3 DISTRICT SIX MUSEUM ★
(129 E5) (*ᗞ H5*)

District Six is the name of a suburb whose sad history is hard to imagine *(see 'In a Nutshell')*. The museum was designed in collaboration with former residents and the story of the destruction of the district covers the walls and everywhere you look there is memorabilia donated by past residents. A replica of one of the homes captures the atmosphere of the neighbourhood as does a huge city map on which former residents have identified the sites of their homes. An ever expanding memory cloth contains their messages. Group tours through the suburb on demand (minimum five persons at 50 rand/person). *Mon 9am–2.30pm, Tue–Sat 9am–4pm, otherwise by appointment only | tel. 021 4 66 72 00 | www.districtsix.co.za | 25 Buitenkant St | Central*

■4 GREENMARKET SQUARE ☺
(129 D4) (*ᗞ G4*)

At some or other point every tourist will land up on this bustling square: the vibe is great, the vendors friendly and you get to choose from a great selection of crafts from all over the African continent including carvings, jewellery, original art made from recycled materials, and hand-made wire radios to name but a few. *Mon–Sat 9am–4pm | Greenmarket Square | Central*

Greenmarket Square – your first stop for local arts and crafts

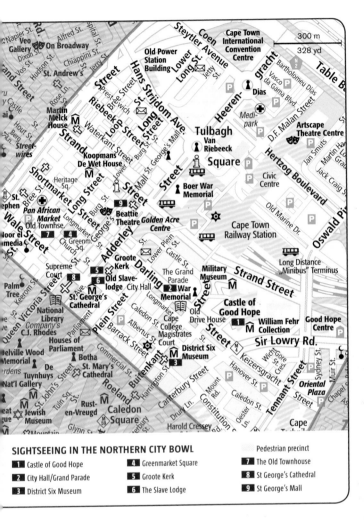

SIGHTSEEING IN THE NORTHERN CITY BOWL

1 Castle of Good Hope

2 City Hall/Grand Parade

3 District Six Museum

4 Greenmarket Square

5 Groote Kerk

6 The Slave Lodge

Pedestrian precinct

7 The Old Townhouse

8 St George's Cathedral

9 St George's Mall

5 GROOTE KERK

(129 D4–5) (ꕤ G4–5)

South Africa's oldest church was completed in 1704. It has two architectural styles, the second of which was as a result of an expansion and renovation in 1836. The tower forms part of the original building. The pulpit resting on the shoulders of two lions dates back to 1798 and is the work of sculptors Anton Anreith and Jan Graaf. The lions were originally painted so true to life that the congregation feared them so they had to be repainted in a plainer colour. The crypt of the church is the final resting place of prominent figures like Simon van der Stel, who governed the Cape 1691. *Mon–Fri 10am–2pm | Adderley St, access from Church Square | Central*

6 **THE SLAVE LODGE** (129 D5) *(Ø G5)*
The VOC's Slave Lodge was built in 1679 and at times more than 500 slaves were packed into its walls. It is the city's second oldest colonial building and was used

Tutu's church – St George's Cathedral

for a number of different purposes over the centuries. Not only slaves and prostitutes were housed here, but from the 19th century, the offices of the govern-ment and at times the high court. Today the Slave Lodge is a museum. Antiques, ceramics, toys, silver and textiles from South Africa's history form part of the permanent collection as do some works by the Khoisan, Cape Town's original in-habitants. Temporary exhibitions are also on display and they are usually about issues like human rights or the interna-tional history of slavery. *Mon–Sat 10am–5pm | www.iziko.org.za/museums/slave-lodge | 49 Adderley St | Central*

7 **THE OLD TOWNHOUSE**
(129 D4) *(Ø G4)*
The city's old town hall, built in 1755, is right on Greenmarket Square. After hav-ing served as the town garrison, an ad-ministrative building and a court house, this rococo style building is now devoted to the arts. It is home to the world famous *Michaelis Collection* – donated by the 19th century mining magnate and patron of the arts Max Michaelis – a collection of Dutch and Flemish masters from the 17th century. *(Mon–Fri 10am–5pm, Sat 10am–4pm | entrance free of charge)*. The white circle on the ground by the entrance is officially the centre of the city. It is from here that all the city's distances are meas-ured. A visit to the INSIDER TIP café in the pretty garden behind the building is a must, as is attending a classical concert in the historic interior. Find out more on site or at tourist information. *Greenmarket Square | Longmarket St | Central*

8 **ST GEORGE'S CATHEDRAL**
(129 D5) *(Ø G5)*
Built in the early 20th century (the foun-dation stone was laid in 1901) this neo-Gothic church is less well known for its architectural style than for its political history: Anglican Archbishop Desmond Tutu – Nobel Peace Prize winner and chairman of the Truth and Reconciliation

Commission that dealt with the crimes committed before the country's transition to democracy – hammered on its doors on 7 September 1986. He did this to send a message of his intention to become the first black archbishop in South Africa's history. Three years later his wish was granted. This church was a bastion of resistance against the apartheid government and while he is no longer the Archbishop he is still held in very high moral esteem by all South Africans. The Cape Town Symphony Orchestra sometimes gives evening performances here – the acoustics are superb! *Open Mon–Fri 8am–5pm, Sat 8am–12.30pm, Sun for church services 7am, 8am, 10am, 11am | tel. 021 4 24 73 60 | www.stgeorgescathedral. com | 1 Wale St | Central*

■9■ ST GEORGE'S MALL
(129 D–E4) (ᗰ G–H4)

This pedestrian zone is Cape Town's business hub, by day office workers can be seen rushing along from one meeting to the next, spending their lunch hour in one of its many coffee shops or buying a snack from a street vendor. However, after hours the pedestrian zone empties so fast you would be forgiven for thinking it is a ghost town, which does make it unsuitable after dark.

WATERFRONT, BO-KAAP & GREEN POINT

The suburbs around the City Bowl all have their own unique character. The jewel is the V&A Waterfront in the harbour, a popular tourist attraction and one of Cape Town's most sought after shopping destinations.

Here you will find some of Cape Town's most expensive hotels and restaurants as well as the Robben Island boat tours pier. Many Capetonians themselves opt to spend their spare time in the malls and movie houses here. Across the way are the colourful houses of the Bo-Kaap neighbourhood, home to Cape Town's Muslim community which in turn abuts the stylish cottages of the De Waterkant area. And there is also Green Point with its many restaurants and cafés and its landmark 2010 Soccer World Cup stadium that changed the face of the suburb forever.

RATHER SAFE THAN SORRY

The security situation in Cape Town has improved notably in recent years. The non-profit Cape Town Partnership brings together public and private shareholders and trained personnel to ensure that the city centre is safe and clean. A network of security cameras have also been set up through the entire city centre. To enjoy a hassle-free holiday, stick to a few simple rules: never walk alone after dark in desolate side streets; only go on a nature trail in a group of at least three people and always leave expensive jewellery and watches behind in your hotel safe. Should something happen to you while on holiday, phone the city tourism authority emergency centre on *107* or *021 4 80 77 00* for assistance.

■1 BO-KAAP ★

(128–129 C–D3) (*Ɱ F3–4*)

This district is more like a Muslim village than a city suburb. It is full of winding, cobbled alleyways, brightly painted houses and mosques. There are a total of eleven mosques, one of which is also South Africa's oldest. The majority of residents are Cape Malay whose families have been living here for generations. In 1834 the first freed slaves settled in the Bo-Kaap and made a living here. The *Bo-Kaap Museum (Mon–Sat 9am–5pm | entrance 10 rand | 71 Wale St)* showcases the history of the neighbourhood and its people with some remarkable pictures. One of the legacies of the days of slavery is the *Cape Town Minstrel Carnival*. Because the slaves had to work on New Year's Day they could only celebrate New Year a few days later. Ever since then bands of musicians have made their way through the streets of Cape Town on the second day

of January. Thousands of people throng to see the processions and while they wait they enjoy the fare served at the many food stalls that are set up along the route. If you would like to get to know the Bo-Kaap better then you should join a INSIDER TIP *Bo-Kaap Cooking Experience*. A local family will take you to a Halaal butchery and spice store before heading back to their home where they will let you in on the secrets of Bo-Kaap cuisine *(tel. 021 7 90 25 92 | www.andulela.com)*.

■2 DE WATERKANT ★

(129 D3) (*Ɱ G3–4*)

The suburb of De Waterkant is also known by Capetonians as the *Cape Quarter* and it is the charmingly beautiful heart of Cape Town's gay community. The Cape Quarter derives its name from an entire block that is home to some of the city's most fashionable interior design stores, designer boutiques and hip bars. And

Bo-Kaap – the colourful Muslim district

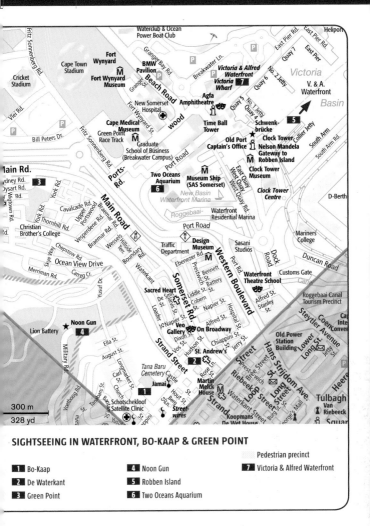

SIGHTSEEING IN WATERFRONT, BO-KAAP & GREEN POINT

1 Bo-Kaap

2 De Waterkant

3 Green Point

4 Noon Gun

5 Robben Island

6 Two Oceans Aquarium

Pedestrian precinct

7 Victoria & Alfred Waterfront

there is little trace today of its red-light district past. It also has plenty of accommodation options ranging from elegant guest houses to boutique hotels, with the suburb's quaint historic cottages particularly popular among visitors *(see 'Where to Stay', p. 80)*. The place has a real holiday village feel to it.

3 GREEN POINT ☼

(128 B–C1) (*ⴅ E–F 1–2*)

Ahead of the decision to build Cape Town's 2010 Soccer World Cup stadium in Green Point, a bitter fight broke out between the city authorities and its residents. The area on which the stadium was finally built was donated as a recreational area to the city of Cape Town by King George V in 1923. The golf course and the old stadium among others had to give way for the new stadium. What has remained is the market. Hundreds of traders set up their stalls here every Sunday morning to sell second-hand goods and arts and crafts *(also see 'Shopping', p. 64)*, as did the Main Road with its fantastic atmosphere and its many boutiques and restaurants. Today the area surrounding the stadium has been turned into a beautifully landscaped park with a wonderful children's playground.

■4 NOON GUN ☼ (128 C3) (⌀ F3)

The tradition of the firing of the Noon Gun at noon every day (except Sundays or public holidays) was started in1806 and has been upheld ever since. At around 11.30am the canon, which is high above the Bo-Kaap neighbourhood, is loaded with more than 3kg/6.6lb of gunpowder. It is then ready to be fired at midday. In the past the cannon salute served as a time signal so that the captains of passing ships could set their chronometers. Today it is more likely a signal that prompts office workers in the city to start thinking about where best they would like to spend their lunch break. *Military Road | Signal Hill (signposted from Buitengracht St)*

■5 ROBBEN ISLAND ★ ●
(U A1) (⌀ a1)

The island in Table Bay is the most poignant reminder of the way in which the apartheid regime treated their opponents. Nelson Mandela served most of his prison sentence here together with other ANC activists for their attempts to overthrow the government. Today it is a place of pilgrimage where visitors get to see his prison cell. The tours are conducted by former prisoners so visitors get first-hand impressions of what prison life was like. The island was declared a Unesco World Heritage Site in 1999. Included in the four-hour

Robben Island – displays tell the history of the former prison

tour is the ferry crossing (approx. 30 minutes each way). Book early to avoid disappointment. *Daily on the hour from 9am–3pm, also 5pm in peak season | tickets 220 rand | tel. 021 413 42 20 | www.robben-island.org.za | Victoria & Alfred Waterfront, Nelson Mandela Gateway at the Clock Tower*

6 TWO OCEANS AQUARIUM ●
(129 D2) (*ω G2*)

Take in the captivating underwater world of both the Indian and the Atlantic Oceans without even setting foot in the water. Visitors with a scuba diving certificate and who want to a bit of a thrill, can even spend an hour INSIDER TIP diving with sharks. During the dive they can come within touching distance of sharks, turtles and rays. Friends and family can watch it all through massive acrylic windows in the visitors' viewing gallery. *Daily 9.30am–6pm | entrance 105 rand, shark dive (including equipment) 595 rand | tel. 021 418 38 23 | www.aquarium.co.za | Victoria & Alfred Waterfront | Dock Road*

7 VICTORIA & ALFRED WATERFRONT
★ ● (129 D–E 1–2) (*ω G–H 1–2*)

The Victoria & Alfred Waterfront is one of the city's major attractions and it certainly warrants a visit, even by those who usually prefer to stay well clear of tourist attractions. The V&A Waterfront area is named after two harbour basins that were named after Victoria, former Queen of England, and her son Alfred. In the 1990s the area was renovated and an entertainment and shopping precinct developed. Today the vast complex has exclusive hotels, stylish boutiques, speciality shops, supermarkets and department stores. Upmarket restaurants and fast food outlets vie for terrace space, while the open-air amphitheatre hosts jazz festivals, local bands and film screenings – there is usually something on a Sunday afternoon. The harbour is a fully functional commercial port so there are fishing boats, yachts and tugboats constantly making their way to or from the high seas, even the occasional cruise ship drops anchor here. The Waterfront is not only popular with tourists, it is also where many Capetonians do their shopping and then go for a stroll among the buskers afterwards, or take in a movie or a meal.

ALSO WORTH A VISIT

CAMPS BAY
(126 A–C 2–4) (*ω B–C 8–9*)

If you look at the spectacular suburb nestled against the Twelve Apostles mountain range it is hard to believe that nobody wanted to settle here until the 20th century. The city's Dutch founding fathers seem to have been totally unimpressed by the beautiful the beaches that are so popular today; they didn't develop the area as it was too far away from the city centre. It is only recently that Camps Bay and neighbouring Clifton developed into a bastion of affluence and beauty. An increasing number of exclusive hotels and luxury villas have sprung up here and today it is only a small minority of Capetonians and wealthy foreigners who can afford to purchase property here, in the shadows of the mountains. The beach promenade is lined with trendy bars and hip restaurants and has a vibe all of its own. ● 'See and be seen' is the category *Café Caprice* would best fall under and its arched terrace is where the city's in-crowd (and visitors who are lucky to find a spot here) enjoy their sundowners while watching the sunset *(daily 9am–11pm | 37 Victoria Road | Camps Bay | tel. 021 4*

38 83 15 | www.cafecaprice.co.za). A city guide once called the long, white beach the 'Côte de Camps Bay' for its European flair. It is also a popular choice for a game of ● beach volleyball, you will also find the city's best ice cream parlour tucked away on the first floor of Promenade Centre **INSIDER TIP** *Sinfull Ice Cream Emporium* which has an unusual selection of delicious flavours *(daily 10am–11.30pm | Shop No. 5, Promenade Centre | Victoria Road)*.

CLIFTON I–IV
(127 D5–6) *(ĸ A–B 6–7)*

Clifton Beach is divided into four sections partly separated from one another by large rocks that jut into the sea. To access the beaches you will have to find parking somewhere on the main road in the stretch between Sea Point and Camps Bay and then climb from the road level down the stairs to the beaches. A word of advice: trying to find parking here, especially on a weekend, can be quite exasperating. The reason why people flock to Clifton in their droves is the unique location nestled as they are between multi-storey buildings and rocks that shelter them from the wind. The suburb is home to some of the most expensive real estate in South Africa.

DEVIL'S PEAK ☀
(U B2) *(ĸ K9)*

Viewed from Cape Town city centre this mountain (just over 1000m/3280ft) has Table Mountain to its left. The best view of it is from *Rhodes Memorial* which is also where its hiking trails start from.

GROOT CONSTANTIA ★ ● ☀ ⏱
(U B3) *(ĸ b3)*

This wine estate in the Constantia valley is South Africa's oldest and the only one that has a museum detailing the history of the Cape, with a particular emphasis on its rich viticulture heritage. You can also take a tour through the wine cellars. The farm was founded in 1685 by Simon van der Stel, who later became governor of the Cape. The valuable furniture, paintings and porcelain in his home have been so well preserved that one has the feeling that he might arrive around the corner any minute and politely ask everyone to leave his living room!

Right next door is one of the two restaurants on the estate: *Jonkershuis (tel. 0217 94 62 55 | Moderate)* where traditional fare like the *Malay Platter* – a combination of Cape Malay delicacies – is served outdoors under the trees. Enjoy the view across the vineyards and where the distant Cape headland blends into the ocean on the horizon. On Sundays (weather permitting) Groot Constantia hosts a small *antiques market* where you can buy old coins, jewellery and books *(10am–4pm)*. Not far off are the smaller but equally charming estates of Buitenverwachting, Constantia Uitsig, Klein Constantia and Steenberg. *Daily 10am–5pm | tel. 0217 94 51 28 | Groot Constantia is centrally located; take the M 3 and M 41 (exit: Constantia) and after 1km turn left to the wine estate*

KIRSTENBOSCH NATIONAL BOTANICAL GARDENS ★ (U B2–3) *(ĸ b2–3)*

This park only 5km/3mi from central Cape Town is a veritable gem. Established in 1895, today it ranks as the one of the most beautiful parks in the world. The diversity of the plant species is overwhelming: more than a third of the 22,000 plants occurring in South Africa grow in Kirstenbosch. From December to April, Cape Town's beloved **INSIDER TIP** summer concerts are performed on its open-air stage. Join the locals and spend an evening listening to South Africa's music greats against the backdrop of Table Mountain while enjoying your picnic and a glass of wine. *Sept–March daily 8am–7pm, April–Aug daily*

Cape Town in bloom – view of Table Mountain from Signal Hill

8am–6pm | entrance fee 32 rand | Rhodes Drive | Newlands

LION'S HEAD & SIGNAL HILL ☼
(127 E5/128 B3) (⟑ C6/E3)

Lion's Head is the perfect place to watch the sun sinking into the Atlantic. Take the M 62 then head towards Signal Hill after 300m you will come across the hiking trail that leads up to Lion's Head. Bank on at least two and a half hours for the hike up and back down and you will need to be fit! The last stretch to the summit has chain ropes and can be quite difficult. If you have an emergency contact *Mountain Rescue* on *tel. 086 110 64 17*. If you decide to skip Lion's Head you can always just drive up Signal Hill. From here you will get a wonderful view of the sea on the one side, the city on the other. This is also where paraglider flights across Camps Bay take off from. A **INSIDER TIP** tandem jump with an experienced pilot can be the experience of a lifetime (*e.g. Para-Taxi | tel. 082 9 66 20 47 | www.para-taxi.com). Kloof Nek Road | signposted on the M 62 between Camps Bay and the city centre*

OBSERVATORY
(131 E–F 4–5) (⟑ N–O 6–7)

This student neighbourhood *(see 'Walking Tours', p. 91)* is also very popular with the international backpacker crowd. The centre of 'Obz', as it is fondly called, is *Lower Main Road* with its cafés, bars and shops. South African comedian, Kurt Schoonraad, who also lives in the neighbourhood, has on occasion jokingly told his audience

Rhodes Memorial – tribute to the diamond magnate and politician

that if you ask someone on the street the time, they will probably answer: 'No idea, maybe winter?' During the day Observatory's inviting street cafés are ideal for a coffee e.g. *Mimi (daily | 107 Lower Main Road)*, then at night you could play a game of pool or go dancing in one of the clubs. The Obz Festival is held once a year, on the first weekend of December, the pubs and cafés set their tables and chairs up in the streets, a stage is set up and everyone who is anyone on the South African music scene entertains in one of South Africa's biggest street festivals.

RHODES MEMORIAL ☀️
(U B2) (*M9*)
This monument, which is modelled on a Greek temple, is just above the University of Cape Town and was built in honour of Cecil Rhodes. He arrived in 1870 as an impoverished 17-year-old and died, aged of 48, as a millionaire. He made his fortune from Kimberley's diamond reserves.

Rhodes was a politician with delusions of grandeur who founded the then Rhodesia (now Zimbabwe) and had granite quarried from Table Mountain for his own memorial. From the memorial you get a spectacular view across the expanse between the inner city and False Bay and on a sunny afternoon the INSIDER**TIP** café next to it is the ideal place to enjoy a cup of tea and a slice of cake *(daily 9am–5pm)*. *Rhodes Drive | Newlands | Groote Schuur Estate (signposted from the M 3 heading out of town)*

INSIDER**TIP** SANDY BAY
(U A3) (*a3*)
Sandy Bay beach lies in relative seclusion and this means that it is quite tranquil here even during weekends and in peak season, which can be a rarity in Cape Town at these times. To reach Sandy Bay continue on the main road that takes you through Camps Bay and then turn right into Llandudno. Once at the beach car

park, take the 20-minute walk on a beaten path until you reach Sandy Bay beach beneath *Little Lion's Head* (the path is signposted). If once you arrive you realise that you have forgotten your swimming costume: no problem at all as you will not be alone – Sandy Bay is Cape Town's unofficial nudist bathing paradise.

SEA POINT
(127 E–F 2–3) (*Ⓜ C–D 3–4*)
Sea Point lies right by the sea and has a very down to earth feel to it. Its beach promenade is lined with one apartment block after another and during the day hooting taxis race along the Main Road on their commute between Camps Bay and the city centre. In its many restaurants and take-away outlets you can sample just about every cuisine in the world. It is also home to a strong Jewish community whose influences can be felt in the shops and businesses. The shore here is rocky so there are no beaches but instead there is a broad promenade along the seaside that is lit up at night by a chain of lights. It is wide enough for everybody and it is a favourite choice for joggers, skaters, cyclists and residents just wanting a seaside stroll. Even though this stretch of coast is not really suitable for swimming, and the water here is very cold, it does not mean you cannot go for a swim. Head to the Sea Point Pavilion at the end of the promenade where you will find INSIDER TIP Cape Town's only saltwater pool *(Oct–March daily 7am–7pm, April–Sept 8.30am–5pm | entrance 9 rand | Beach Road)*.

TABLE MOUNTAIN ★ ● ☼
(U B2) (*Ⓜ D–L 8–12*)
There are numerous paths and hikes that lead up Cape Town's landmark – at least 500 – but most visitors opt to take the cable car from Kloof Nek. If you plan to hike up, pick up a trail map at the V&A Waterfront Information Centre at the Clock Tower or at the Kirstenbosch Visitor Information Centre before you set out. Kirstenbosch is also where INSIDER TIP the most beautiful hike starts out from. Depending on how fit you are the *Skeleton Gorge* trail can take anything between two to three hours. It is mostly in the shade and it takes you via *Smuts Track* to *Maclears Beacon.* Be sure to exercise extreme caution

FLYOVER TO NOWHERE

Cape Town's famous white elephant is right in the middle of the city: an unfinished section of motorway that crosses over the busy intersection at Buigtengracht Street. A flyover that leads to nowhere. Construction on the motorway was stalled back in the 1960s and the incomplete bridge remains to this day. There are a number of urban myths about why it has never been completed. They range from miscalculations by the engineers that would prevent the sections from joining, to stories of a shop owner who refused to sell his property and so blocked its path and the popular belief that the city simply ran out of money. The most likely reason is that it was a preparatory structure put in place for future completion when the road network needed to be expanded. Cape Town's peak hour traffic is bursting at the seams but the landmark remains. Today it is a popular location for photo shoots and movies.

if it starts to rain, there are wooden pathways on some sections and they can become extremely slippery. *Platteklip Gorge* is another popular trail. It begins a few hundred metres from the cable car station in Kloof Nek. The gorge is narrow and the hike up is steep, which means your route to the top is very direct. Hiking boots are essential as is a day pack as it is very important that you take a trail map, ample water, energy snacks, sun protection and weather gear – the weather can change very quickly. Be sure that your mobile phone is adequately charged so that you can at least make an emergency call to *Mountain Rescue (tel. 021 9 48 99 00)* or *Kirstenbosch security (tel. 021 7 99 86 18)*. From the summit you will have a breathtaking view across Cape Town's sprawling suburbs, the sea and the distant mountains. With a bit of luck you will even come across some animals: *dassies* (rock hyraxes) are the most likely but you may also see mountain goats, ibex and baboons. If you have come up by cable car then you take a stroll on one of the demarcated paths to the viewing points. The cable car operating times are seasonal and weather dependent. The first car could take you up as early as 7.30am, the last leaves at 8.30pm. To avoid the long queues

INSIDER **TIP** book your tickets online for only ten rand more than what you would pay at the booth *(return ticket 195 rand | tel. 021 4 24 81 81 | www.tablemountain. net). Table Mountain Road*

TOWNSHIPS

There are seven official townships in addition to many more informal settlements on the outskirts of Cape Town. You often hear the term *Cape Flats* when referring to townships because many of them are located on the flat sandy stretch between Table Mountain and False Bay. Among the townships are Gugulethu, Khayelitsha (South Africa's second largest with 300,000 residents) and Langa (the oldest). The living conditions in the townships are vast and varied. There is a mixture of old and new, affluent and poor. Some live in low-cost housing with running water and electricity while others live in shacks without running water or electricity. Because of the population explosion in the past few years, the infrastructure being built can no longer keep up and there are real issues around overcrowding. The city administration is doing what it can to provide homes for everybody. To experience what life in the townships is like take an organised tour like

KEEP FIT!

● The perfect training ground to prepare you for rock climbing in the great outdoors is the *CityROCK Indoor Climbing Centre* in Observatory. On-site trainers will literally teach you the ropes and here the challenge is on even for advanced climbers. There is a shop selling all the necessary outdoor climbing equipment and a fitness studio in the complex. A trial course will cost you 190 rand. *Mon–Fri 9am–noon, Fri 9am–6pm, Sat/ Sun 10am–6pm | Collingwood St (131 F5) (瓜 O6) | Observatory | tel. 021 4 47 13 26 | www.cityrock. co.za*

Making a living from pottery – a workshop in Nyanga township

INSIDER TIP *Bonani Tours (tel. 021 5 31 42 91 | www.bonanitours.co.za)* one of several operators offering the service. Small groups are taken to visit schools, African traditional healers, township pubs and you get to interact with the locals. There are two important reasons why a township tour is recommended. Firstly, you get to meet the Capetonians you would never get a chance to meet in the areas on the beach or in restaurants and secondly, the township residents benefit from the proceeds of tourism to their areas.

INSIDER TIP THE HEART OF CAPE TOWN MUSEUM
(131 D–E 5–6) (*M–N7*)

Towering over the suburb of Observatory is the imposing Groote Schuur Hospital. Floodlit at night, this is where heart surgeon Professor Chris Barnard performed the world's first heart transplant in 1967. His patient only lived for 18 days but he now world famous as the pioneer of a whole new discipline in medicine. Today the famous heart is on exhibit at the Heart of Cape Town Museum as is the same operating theatre where the groundbreaking surgery was performed. On display are media and press clippings, letters and other historical documents. *Tours daily 9am, 11am, 1pm, 3pm, 5pm | 200 rand | www.heartofcapetown.co.za | Main Road | Observatory (Old Main Building, Groote Schuur Hospital)*

TWELVE APOSTLES
(U A–B 2–3) (*a–b 2–3*)

The Twelve Apostles mountain range stretches from the back of Table Mountain in a southerly direction. The rugged terrain is unsuitable for hikes so a far better option is to lie on the beaches below and view their peaks with the sound of the sea in the background.

TRIPS & TOURS

BLOUBERGSTRAND (U B1) (*m b1*)

Only 30km/18.6mi from central Cape Town are the beaches of Bloubergstrand. The suburb owes its Afrikaans name to its spectacular view of Table Mountain that is bathed in a blue haze as the sun down. Go out there for the day, pack a swimming costume and then stay to enjoy one of the Cape's most spectacular sunsets.

It is a good idea to head there in the morning so you have a full day at the beach. Take the N 1 from the city centre then turn off to the R 27 towards *Milnerton*. If you happen to make the drive on a weekend you will pass a popular seaside flea market on your left *(see 'Shopping', p. 64).*

Stop for a browse or take the path to the beach behind the dunes, it is usually far too windy to stay for a swim but it is a good place to watch the kitesurfers as they fly through the Atlantic surf with Table Mountain as their backdrop. Back on the road again travel until you reach Blaauwberg Road then turn left towards the sea. When you reach the traffic circle and see all the kitesurfers you know you have arrived at *Bloubergstrand* ● this is where kitesurf professionals from all over the world do their training from December to March. So find a parking place along the beach to enjoy the spectacle.

The best swimming beach is further along at Big Bay. Back at the traffic circle take

BOOKS & FILMS

▶ **Long Walk to Freedom** – The story of Nelson Mandela is closely intertwined with the history of this country. He was one of few leaders who was able to unite South Africa's different races behind him. This moving autobiography will give you a better insight when you visit some of the sites like Robben Island and the Grand Parade that formed an integral part of his journey.

▶ **Disgrace** – This multi-award winning book by Nobel literature laureate J. M. Coetzee gives the reader an in-depth insight into the racial problems that still exist in South Africa today.

▶ **The Good Doctor** – Published in 2003 and shortlisted for a number of prestigeious book prizes, this novel by Damon Galgut is a parable about an idealistic young doctor in a neglected rural hospital in post-apartheid South Africa.

▶ **U-Carmen eKhayelithsa** – This film adaptation of Georges Bizet's opera transposes the story of Carmen into Cape Town's biggest township. In 2005 it was awarded the Golden Bear at the Berlinale, the international film festival in Berlin.

▶ **Yesterday** – This 2004 film became the first Zulu language film in South Africa that made it to the international big screen. It tells the moving and harrowing tale of a woman infected with the Aids virus by her husband and her final wish in life is to be able to live long enough to see her daughter go to school.

the exit away from Table Mountain and along the beach. At the next traffic circle turn left (signpost Big Bay). Here there is often very little or no wind at all and it is perfect for a day at the beach plus you get a wonderful view of Table Mountain

For an alternative to a *Blue Peter* pizza there is the fine dining option of *On the Rocks (Mon–Fri noon–10pm, Sat/Sun 9am–10pm | 45 Stadler Rd | tel. 021 5 54 19 88 | Moderate)*. The fish dishes come highly recommended and it is best to

Sunset becomes an event at the Blue Peter Hotel in Bloubergstrand

from here. Once the sun begins to set the view is even more awe-inspiring and you should really enjoy it with a glass of wine in hand. A good spot for this on the INSIDER TIP hotel lawn in front of the *Blue Peter (daily noon–10pm | Popham Road | tel. 021 5 54 19 56)* which attracts locals and holiday-makers alike for sundowners. On balmy summer evenings its patrons happily spill out on to the lawn if the tables and benches are taken. Capetonians and visitors alike – a tasty slice of pizza in one hand and a glass of wine in the other – all toast another glorious day as the spectacle of Table Mountain at dusk unfolds before them.

reserve a window table where you can see the view of the distant city through the sea spray. The perfect end to a perfect day.

FALSE BAY
(U B 4–5) (*Ø b4–5*)
This trip takes you through False Bay's charming coastal villages to the penguin colony near the southernmost point of the route: approximately 40km/25mi.
Take the M 3 out of Cape Town through the beautiful Constantia valley in the direction of Muizenberg. ☀ At the end of this stretch you will have a fantastic view of False Bay. For some early seafarers

this view was a bitter disappointment: it meant that they had turned too early and were in the 'false bay' instead of the correct bay at Cape Town.

Muizenberg is a popular beach destination especially since the seawater is far warmer here than on the other side of the peninsula. For years the buildings here were left in disrepair, giving the once popular holiday resort town a hint of a ghost town. However, slowly but surely it is awaking from its slumber and recent years have seen it undergo an urban revival. The beach goers that flock here come from all walks of life, in contrast to the trendy crowds on Camps Bay and Clifton beaches. Many come here **INSIDER TIP** to learn to surf. The waves here are ideal for beginners and not as big as elsewhere on the peninsula. Perfect for those first attempts to stand up and if you cannot get the hang of it here, then you never will! *Gary's Surf School (34 Beach Rd | tel. 021 7 88 98 39)* hires out surfboards and wetsuits and offers lessons for beginners. Only swim where there are lifeguards and follow their instructions. A hundred or so sharks can turn up here every year but there are now shark spotters on duty on the mountain as an early warning system. As you carry on along the coast in the direction of Kalk Bay, you will pass through *St James* with its old fashioned, brightly coloured wooden changing cabins. The cabins have become a landmark of sorts for False Bay and are an ideal photo opportunity. Their bright colours epitomise the entire spectrum of the rainbow nation that makes use of them today (unlike in the past). This stretch of coast also has a number of lovely ● tidal pools.

Kalk Bay, the next town on the trip was settled as early at the 17th century because its natural harbour made it possible to launch fishing boats. The village became the base for a thriving fishing industry that still continues to this day. The village derives its name from the Dutch word for lime which was extracted here from seashells and used in the construction of buildings. The British arrived here in the early 19th century and established a whaling station. In later years it became a popular summer resort for the wealthy. In the decades after the 1920s a construction slump meant that hardly any new homes were built so the beautiful old homes and buildings from its heyday remain to this day. The Main Road is lined with antique shops, boutiques, art galleries and quaint cafés like the *Olympia Café and Deli (daily | 134 Main Rd)* which is a good option for

RELAX & ENJOY

Treat your aching muscles to a professional massage with therapist ● Eslinah Magemgenene who lost her eyesight in 1993 through illness. Despite the new challenges this presented in her life she refused to let her handicap get the better of her. Today she runs a successful massage therapy studio in Newlands and 180 rand an hour is very reasonable at today's prices *(tel. 021 6 89 51 26 | 43 Dean Street* **(0)** *(㎞ N11–12) | Newlands)*. For a different kind of massage you can try ● *Equinox Spa* which specialises in Swedish Massage techniques from northern Europe using warm soya candle wax *(tel. 021 4 30 05 12 | 47 Main Road* **(128 B2)** *(㎞ E2) | Green Point)*.

you to have your breakfast before you start to explore.

A visit to the harbour is an experience in itself. In the afternoon, the fishing boats return to the harbour with their catches. The *Harbour House (daily noon–4pm, 6pm–10pm | tel. 021 7 88 41 33 | Moderate)* is a lovey fish restaurant and *The Polana,*

pass through *Simon's Town*, the Cape's naval base. Victorain town houses line the main road and The Quayside – a mini waterfront – is the town's tourist centre. Just after Simon's Town is *The Boulders* beach turn-off to a 3000-strong penguin colony that had its beginnings with just two breeding pairs that settled here in

The brightly coloured changing cabins at St James on False Bay

a charming bar – with amazing views – serves Portuguese cuisine. It is open until the early hours but best to check what time the kitchen closes *(Sun–Thu 4.30pm–1am, Fri/Sat 4.30pm–3am, also open for lunch in summer | tel. 021 7 88 71 62)*. A little further along the route, at Glencairn, guide Jenni Trethowan offers organised hikes to INSIDER TIP troops of wild baboons that live on the mountains above the coast *(250 rand | tel. 021 7 82 20 15)*. Now drive further south to the penguin colony at *The Boulders*. En route you will

1982. The colony goes about its daily business undeterred by the curious onlookers – you can even swim with them *(Dec/Jan daily 7am–7.30pm, Feb–March daily 8am–6pm, April–Nov daily 8am–5pm | 35 rand | tel. 021 7 86 23 29)*.

CAPE OF GOOD HOPE ★
(U B6) (∅ b6)

It is a good idea to set off early in the morning. It is 60km/37mi to the *Cape of Good Hope* and you want to be able to spend some unhurried time here. The return trip also includes some not to be missed opportunities: horseback riding on the beach at *Noordhoek* and a ride along the scenic *Chapman's Peak Drive*, followed by a dinner of freshly caught fish in *Hout Bay* harbour. Start the trip in the early morning so that you will have the quiet morning hours to enjoy the Cape itself. Take the M 3 towards Muizenberg and follow the directions to Cape Point. Plan to spend the rest of the morning until lunchtime at the *Cape of Good Hope Table Mountain National Park* – justifiably one of the region's most popular tourist destinations *(Nov–Jan daily 6am–8pm, Feb–April, Aug–Oct 7am–7pm, May–July 8am–6pm | 55 rand | www.tmnp.co.za)*.

The 20,000 acre reserve is home to zebras, baboons, antelopes and ostriches and is rich in indigenous fynbos plants. With a

little patience you may be able see a few of them from your car or if you go on one of the many hikes. Sadly, most visitors head straight to the funicular at the end of the park. The ride takes you up to the old lighthouse at *Cape Point*, or almost, as there are still over a hundred stairs to climb. It is well worth the climb for the expansive views of the peninsula, the wild Atlantic below and the new lighthouse perched on the rocks. The other mandatory photo stop for most visitors is the *Cape of Good Hope* beacon. To get your bearings in the park or to find its hidden sandy beaches or go on a hike (shortest is 40 minutes but some can be up to two hours) it is a good idea to stop off at the *Buffelsfontein Visitor Centre (signposted halfway between the park entrance and Cape Point | tel. 021 7 80 92 04)* before you head out.

Around 3000 penguins at the Boulders Beach colony near Simon's Town

FOOD & DRINK

Cape Town's cuisine is as varied as it is unusual. You can taste your way through a spectrum of specialities from throughout Africa, indulge in Indian curries and discover the Cape Malay delights that Cape Town is famous for – a fusion of Malay and European food culture – but this is by no means where the city's food repertoire ends.

The distinctive spices of Southeast Asia are characteristic of the Cape Malay cuisine but the cuisines of Africa, Europe and India are as just as prominent. What makes Cape Town's restaurants so exciting is the inventiveness of its chefs. They combine African influences with European recipes and so they may prepare a steak with a basting of dark chocolate and chilli or serve a pizza with a butternut squash topping, again a typical ingredient of Cape Malay cuisine. And of course you can immediately tell from the menus that Cape Town is by the sea: its fishing boats bring in a fantastic selection of seafood making it a pleasure for Cape Town's chefs to prepare an endless repertoire of delicious fish dishes. Foodies will definitely get their money's worth in the Cape as even the most exclusive restaurants, with well known chefs and exceptional service, are reasonably priced. The Cape's excellent wines are also extremely affordable. Those res-

Photo: Melissa's café and deli

Be wary of the baboons, the reserve is home to five troops, if you are near a troop you should not unpack your food as you risk having it torn from your hands. Intentionally feeding them is expressly prohibited and punishable with a fine.

Once you have enjoyed the diversity of the Cape of Good Hope reserve drive back along the beautiful west coast via *Scarborough* and *Kommetjie* towards *Noordhoek*. Here you can INSIDER TIP explore miles of beach on horseback. This pristine stretch of beach is popular with surfers but it is best to stay in the saddle because swimming in such isolation on a weekday is not safe *(Imhoff Farm | horseback riding from 300 rand for approx. two hours | daily 9am, noon, 4pm | on the M 65, approx. 5 km/3 mi from the M 64 | tel. 021 7 83 11 68 or 082 7 74 11 91).*

The next part of the route is on the particularly scenic 🌿 *Chapman's Peak Drive (32 rand per car)* which connects Noordhoek with Hout Bay. It is a 10km/6mi long winding coastal road with spectacular views. The road works began in 1915 and after years of blasting into the mountain (some 150 m/490ft above sea level) the resultant road, hewn into the rocks, is the Cape's most famous and panoramic. The views from here across to the beaches of Noordhoek, Hout Bay and the open sea are unrivalled. *Chapman's Peak Drive* is occasionally closed during winter for repair work or due to bad weather. An alternative route is the M 64 through the *Silvermine Nature Reserve,* M 3 and M 63 to *Hout Bay.*

Hout Bay is where the coastal route ends. *T'Houtbaaitjen* is Dutch and means 'bay of wood' and is the name given to it by pioneer Jan van Riebeeck in 1652. However, despite its name Hout Bay's livelihood is based on the fishing industry and has little to do with forestry. You should get here in time to take a sunset cruise out to see the seals on *Duiker Island (e.g. Circle Launches | tel. 021 7 90 10 40 | www.circle-launches.co.za or Nauticat Charters | tel. 021 7 90 72 78 | www.nauticatcharters.co.za | approx. 38 rand).*

Worked up an appetite for dinner? Then head to *Mariner's Wharf* Hout Bay's most famous restaurant. The waitrons are dressed as sailors and the seafood is priced for the tourist *(daily 9am–10.30pm | Harbour Road | tel. 021 7 90 11 00 | Moderate).* For a more authentic option try some fish and chips from *Fish on The Rocks* tucked away at the end of Harbour Road *(daily 10.30am–8.30pm | Harbour Road | tel. 021 7 90 00 01 | Budget).* After dinner follow the signs back to Cape Town, the road will take you straight to *Camps Bay's* beach promenade – perfect for that cocktail to end a perfect day.

THE F

DALY BREAD

Bold and adventurous cuisine: Cape Town's chefs use recipes from around the world to conjure up innovative new menus

taurants that do not have a liquor licence will let you bring along your own wine and will only charge a nominal corkage fee, usually between 20–30 rand per bottle. And if you don't finish the bottle then you are welcome to take the rest of the bottle back home with you. The same goes for a meal that you cannot finish, restaurants are happy to pack this up for you to take away as a doggy bag.

Along with the local Chardonnay, Shiraz and Pinotage (unique to South Africa), beer is also a popular accompaniment to any meal especially local brew 'Castle Lager' and Namibian 'Windhoek Lager'. And to round off your meal you should try a digestif like the famous KWV estate's brandy from Paarl. Eating out is very popular in Cape Town so if you have earmarked a restaurant you would like to

The perfect spot for afternoon tea – the Mount Nelson Hotel terrace

try then it is a good idea to reserve a table. There are so many good ones that you really ought to try a new restaurant every evening.

BIRDS CAFÉ (128 C5) (🛍 F5)

Sounds of twittering birds form the backdrop to this eclectic café with its swan shaped lamps suspended from the ceiling. A designer's haven in which the owner has given free reign to her creativity and whose apple strudel will have you coming back for more! *Mon–Fri 7am–4pm, Sat 8am–2pm | 127 Bree St | Central | tel. 021 4 26 25 34*

CAFÉ GAINSBOURG (128 C6) (🛍 F6)

Just the spot to relax with a cappuccino in the afternoon or a glass of wine in the evening. *Mon–Fri 7.30am–10.30pm, Sat/ Sun 8.30am–10.30pm | 64 Kloof St | Gardens | tel. 021 4 22 17 80*

FRIEDA'S (129 D3) (🛍 G3)

Serving delicious sandwiches this lovely 1950s style café is a great choice for a rainy day! Take your book and relax with a cup of tea at one of their old wooden tables. *Mon/Tue 6.30am–4pm, Wed–Fri 6.30am–9pm, Sat 8.30am–1pm | 15 Bree St | Central | tel. 021 4 21 24 04*

GIOVANNI'S (128 B2) (🛍 E2)

If gourmet ham is your thing then *Giovanni's*, opposite the Soccer World Cup stadium in Greenpoint, is for you. Here you will find a wide selection of speciality foods, the country's most important newspapers and an excellent espresso. The beach promenade is only five minutes away and a good idea is to order an extra baguette with your favourite deli filling to go. *Daily 7.30am–9pm | 103 Main Road | Green Point | tel. 021 4 34 68 93*

MELISSA'S (128 C6) (🛍 E–F6)

A café serving excellent pastries and delicious home-made delicacies, it is almost impossible not to leave here with a shopping bag of sinful delights. *Mon–Fri 7.30am–8pm, Sat/So 8am–8pm | 94 Kloof St | Gardens | tel. 021 4 24 55 40*

MOUNT NELSON (128 C5) (*Ϻ F5*)

One of Cape Town's most stylish hotels serves a sumptuous *high tea* every afternoon to residents and guests alike. The spread includes delicious sandwiches and INSIDERTIP **a wide variety of delicate cakes** laid out in a generous buffet *(150 rand)* to the accompaniment of piano music on weekends. Bookings essential. *Daily 2.30pm–5.30pm | 76 Orange St | Gardens | tel. 021 4 83 10 00*

INSIDERTIP MZOLI'S PLACE
(U C2) (*Ϻ c2*)

This is not really a café, but a popular township restaurant in Gugulethu. Well worth a visit because as a tourist you get to mingle with township residents. Get a reputable tour guide to accompany you and it is best not to stay beyond the afternoon to avoid any unnecessary risk. *Mon–Fri 9am–6.30pm, Sat/Sun 9am–8pm | Shop 3 | NY 115 Street | Gugulethu | tel. 021 6 38 13 55*

ORIGIN (129 D3) (*Ϻ G3*)

At *Origin* coffee is elevated to an art work. If the countless blends leave you baffled there is always the barista academy next door for an introductory course into the world of coffee. The coffee is roasted on the premises and there are also more than 100 teas on offer. *Mon–Fri 7am–5pm, Sat 9am–2pm | 28 Hudson Street | Central | tel. 021 4 21 10 00*

LA PETITE TARTE (129 D3) (*Ϻ G3*)

Parisian pavement café culture at its Capetonian best: in the heart of the Cape Quarter. The *tarte tartin* and *croques monsieur* come highly recommended. *Mon–Fri 8.30am–4.30pm, Sat 8.30am–3pm | 5 Shop 11A, Cape Quarter | De Waterkant Street | Central | tel. 021 4 25 90 77*

THE SIDEWALK CAFÉ ● (O) (*Ϻ H7*)

The café with lots of heart! Heart décor – suspended from the ceiling, leaning against antiques and stickers on the windows – and delicious cooking that is straight from the heart. An absolute must for its amazing cuisine! *Mon–Sat 8am–10pm, Sun 9am–2pm | 33 Derry St | Vredehoek | www.sidewalk.co.za | tel. 021 4 61 28 39*

RESTAURANTS: EXPENSIVE

AUBERGINE (129 D6) (*Ϻ G6*)

Enjoy Aubergine's contemporary cuisine from their historic old church pews. The menu and service won't disappoint – either à la carte or a degustation menu – and the knowledgable sommelier will take you through the extensive wine list.

⭐ **Azure**
Fine dining with a spectacular view of the Atlantic → p. 58

⭐ **The Africa Café**
Showcases the entire continent's culinary fare → p. 59

⭐ **Khaya Nyama**
Why not give grilled crocodile a try? → p. 60

⭐ **Fork**
It all happens at Cape Town's trendy tapas bar → p. 59

⭐ **Pigalle**
Sophisticated and very popular with the locals → p. 61

MARCO POLO HIGHLIGHTS

Mon–Sat 7pm–10pm, Wed–Fri also noon–2pm | 39 Barnet St | Gardens | tel. 0214 65 49 09 | www.aubergine.co.za

AZURE ★ (126 A6) (*ш A11*)

The terrace of the *Twelve Apostles* hotel in Camps Bay has to be one of Cape Town's best venues for dinner. The indigenous fynbos grown in the garden also influences the menu flavours – highly recommended. *Daily 7.30am–10.30am, 12.30pm–3.30pm, 6pm–10pm | Twelve Apostles Hotel | Victoria Rd | Oudekraal | tel. 021 4 37 90 29*

GOURMET RESTAURANTS

La Colombe (U B3) (*ш b3*)

Located on the *Constantia Uitsig* wine estate in the Constantia Valley (a 20 minute drive from the city) is one of South Africa's best restaurants. Multi award-winning chef Luke Dale-Roberts of *La Colombe* will tantalise your taste buds with his Asian take on French cuisine. Set menu approx. 625 rand per person. *Daily 12.30pm–2.30pm, 7.30pm–9.30pm | Spaanschemat River Road | Constantia | tel. 021 7 94 23 90*

Constantia Uitsig (U B3) (*ш b3*)

Also located on *Constantia Uitsig* estate but in the old manor house, Italian cuisine with an Asian flare is the hallmark of chef extraordinaire Frank Swainston. Set menu approx. 315 rand per person. *Daily noon–2.30pm, 7pm–9.30pm | Spaanschemat River Road | Constantia | tel. 021 7 94 44 80*

The Greenhouse (U B3) (*ш b3*)

Recent winner of the Restaurant of the Year Award, this exclusive restaurant is located in an historic building in the Cellars-Hohenort Hotel in the Constantia wine lands. Acclaimed chef, Peter Tempelhoff's innovative cuisine promises an exceptional dining experience. Set menu approx. 450 rand per person. *Tue–Sat 7pm–9.30pm | Cellars-Hohenort Hotel | Brommersvlei Rd | Constantia| tel. 021 7 94 21 37*

95 Keerom (129 D5) (*ш G5*)

A stylish Italian restaurant set in the shade of a 100 year old olive tree – try their sensational gnocchi. Set menu approx. 315 rand per person. *Mon–Sat 7pm–11pm, Thu/Fri also noon–2pm | 95 Keerom St | Central | tel. 021 4 22 07 65*

Nobu (129 D1) (*ш G2*)

This is celebrity chef Nobu Matsuhisa's first Nobu in Africa and third internationally, it serves a contemporary menu which blends classical Japanese cuisine with South African specialities. *Mon–Sun from 6pm | in the One&Only | Dock Rd | Waterfront | tel. 021 4 31 51 11*

Planet Restaurant (128 C5) (*ш F5*)

This is the *Mount Nelson Hotel's* restaurant and its specialities include ostrich carpaccio with butternut. Every month a *Wine & Dine* is held and a different estate is invited to showcase its wines. The menu for this (375 rand per person) event is designed to complement the wines. *Planet Bar* is worth a stop afterwards. Set menu approx. 315 rand per person. *Daily 6.30pm–10.30pm | Mount Nelson Hotel | 76 Orange St | Gardens | tel. 021 4 83 19 48*

The Africa Café – the culinary diversity of Africa all on a plate

BUKHARA (129 D4) (*M G4*)

This is Cape Town's best Indian restaurant, taste the curry and you will think you are in Delhi. *Mon–Sat noon–3pm, 6pm–11pm, Sun 6pm–10.30pm | 33 Church St | Central | tel. 021 4 24 00 00 | www.bukhara.com*

SAVOY CABBAGE RESTAURANT & CHAMPAGNE BAR (129 D4) (*M G4*)

Not a year goes by without the *Savoy Cabbage* walking away with yet another award. The chef here prepares the humble cabbage in a different way every day – cabbage has never been this glamorous. *Mon–Fri noon–2pm, Mon–Sat 7pm–10.30pm | 101 Hout St | Central | tel. 021 4 24 26 26*

RESTAURANTS: MODERATE

THE AFRICA CAFÉ ★ (129 D4) (*M G4*)

One of the most charming places for you to discover the pleasures of the African cuisine. To start off with you are served small portions from a buffet with dishes from the north (like Tunisia) all the way to South Africa. Then you make your selection and order your preferred dishes. *Daily 6pm–11pm | 108 Shortmarket St | Central | tel. 021 4 22 02 21 | www.africacafe.co.za*

INSIDER TIP BOMBAY BICYCLE CLUB (0) (*M E6*)

If you are counting on a quiet dinner, this is hardly the place for you. It is precisely its bustling vibe that draws Capetonians to the *Bombay Bicycle Club*. Its atmosphere is reminiscent of carnival, and the décor of a London gentlemen's club and by about ten thirty everyone will be up dancing to Gloria Gaynor. *Mon–Sat 6pm–2am | 158 Kloof St | Central | tel. 021 4 23 68 05*

FORK ★ (129 D4) (*M G4*)

This Long Street establishment is currently *the* restaurant in Cape Town. Rough walls, contemporary big city ambiance and an imaginative selection of delicious tapas. Try the cheese fondue – although it does come at a price, it is well worth it. *Mon–Sat*

RESTAURANTS: MODERATE

noon–11pm | 84 Long St | Central | tel. 021 4 24 63 34 | www.fork-restaurants.co.za

JEWEL TAVERN (129 D4) (*Ⅲ G4*)
Once upon a time the *Jewel Tavern* was the best kept secret among Asian seafarers. Today this gem has its pride of place in Cape Town's restaurant scene. Its authentic Chinese cuisine, especially the fish dishes, comes highly recommended. *Daily 11am–2.30pm, 6pm–10pm | 101 St George's Mall | Central | tel. 021 4 48 19 77*

KHAYA NYAMA ★ (129 D5) (*Ⅲ F–G5*)
This 'house of meat' – as the translation goes – truly does live up to its name. The menu has the whole spectrum of African meat ranging from crocodile to springbok and ostrich. It serves the best game in Cape Town. *Daily 6pm–10.30pm | 267 Long St | Central | tel. 021 4 24 29 17*

MANO'S (128 C2) (*Ⅲ F2*)
Just the place for a relaxing lunch or dinner! The menu is simple and the food delicious: rump or pepper steak with fries and a salad. Then move on to their cocktail bar afterwards to plan the rest of your day or evening. *Mon–Sat noon–11pm | 39 Main Rd | Green Point | tel. 021 4 34 10 90*

NOVA (128 C5) (*Ⅲ F5*)
Beef fillet served with a creamy spinach emulsion and a frozen Béarnaise sauce? This is where Cape Town's top chef, Richard Carstens, serves up his own special style of molecular cuisine. *Relish*, the bar upstairs has a magnificent view of Table Mountain (illuminated at night) making it ideal for a nightcap. *Mon–Sat 7pm–10pm | 70 New Church St | Tamboerskloof | tel. 021 4 22 35 85*

INSIDER TIP PANAMA JACK'S
(131 D2) (*Ⅲ M4*)
This popular fish tavern is right on the dock in the midst of warehouses and serves freshly caught fish bought right off the fishing boats. The drive alone though Cape Town's commercial harbour is as well worth it. *Sun–Fri 12.30pm–3pm and daily 6.30pm–11pm | Quay 500 | Harbour | tel. 021 4 47 39 92*

PEPPER CLUB ON THE BEACH
(126 A3) (*Ⅲ B9*)
You get to choose your own fish or cut of meat at the counter before it is prepared for you. A relaxed and sophisticated gem on Camps Bay's beach promenade. *Daily noon–11.30pm | Victoria Rd | Camps Bay | tel. 021 4 38 31 74*

LOW BUDGET

▶ With its slogan 'Fresh Food Fast' *Crush* is a favourite and affordable lunchtime sandwich restaurant. *Mon–Fri 7am–5pm | 100 St George's Mall* **(129 D4)** (*Ⅲ G4*) | tel. 021 4 22 55 33

▶ For the health conscious there is *Kauai* that serves light meals like a teriyaki chicken wholewheat sandwich and a fresh beetroot juice! The smoothies are delicious. Ask for a bonus card so that you can to collect points for a free smoothie or shake. *34 b Long St* **(129 E4)** (*Ⅲ G4*) | tel. 021 4 21 56 42

▶ *Mohamad's Boerewors Stand* is an institution on Long Street **(129 D5)** (*Ⅲ F–G5*). He sets up his *boerewors* stand in the upper third of Long Street every evening. Club-goers queue up even before he gets there, he uses his own spices and sells the *boerewors* for 10 rand apiece.

LA PERLA (127 E2) (*C4*)

Watch the ocean splash against the shore and the parade of life go by from the terrace of this Sea Point institution. A joking and charming head waiter serves you the cuisine that is as stylish as the ambiance. *Daily 11am–11pm | Beach Road | Sea Point | tel. 021 4 39 95 38*

WAKAME ☆ (O) (*E1*)

Baby spinach with pawpaw; ostrich meat served with asparagus on wasabi cheese; pineapple carpaccio with a lime chili sauce. The chefs here are very serious about their fusion cuisine and you won't mind waiting a little longer when there is so much creativity going on. The wait is made

Guests at Camps Bay's Pepper Club enjoy a perfect beach view while they dine

PIGALLE ★ (129 D3) (*G3*)

A favourite among Capetonians of all ages. After indulging in its sumptuous Portuguese fare – fish is the speciality – the older generation stay on to enjoy a brandy, while the younger ones move on to the bar or the dance floor. *Mon–Sat noon–3pm, 7pm–11pm | 57 A Somerset Road | Green Point | tel. 021 4 21 48 48*

THEO'S GRILL & BUTCHER ☆ (128 A1) (*D2*)

A sophisticated steak restaurant on the Mouille Point promenade that also serves a variety of excellent seafood and salads. *Daily 11am–11pm | 163 Beach Rd | Mouille Point | tel. 021 4 39 34 94*

easier by the splendid sea view from the first floor terrace. *Mon–Thu noon–3pm, 6pm–10.30pm, Fri–Sun 12.30pm–3.30pm, 6pm–11pm | corner Beach Rd/Surrey Place | Mouille Point | tel. 021 4 33 23 77*

RESTAURANTS: BUDGET

BIESMIELLAH (128 C4) (*F4*)

Good Indian and Cape Malay fare is served here and the setting – plastic table cloths, Indian kitsch on the walls and an adjoining corner shop – most certainly belies the food. It is a Muslim restaurant so be aware that no alcohol is served. *Mon–Sat noon–10pm | corner Wale St/Pentz St | Bo-Kaap | tel. 021 4 23 08 50*

LOCAL SPECIALITIES

▶ **Biltong** – air dried beef or game; a traditional snack best bought in the speciality shops found in most malls and tourist areas

▶ **Bobotie** – a slightly sweet (with apricots and raisins) Cape Malay dish of curried minced lamb topped with an egg and milk custard and then baked

▶ **Boerewors** – spiced sausage of the *boers* (farmers) made with beef, pork or lamb (or a combination of these) and best prepared on a *braai*. The city's street vendors sell them in a hot dog roll with fried onions – a popular snack among Long Street's night owls

▶ **Crayfish** – a type of lobster that is freshly caught in the Cape and still reasonably priced for the visitor even after recent price hikes (photo left)

▶ **Game** – especially popular are the various species of antelope e.g. kudu, springbok (South Africa's national animal) or eland – the biggest of the antelope species

▶ **Karoo lamb** – the unique flavour of this lamb comes as no surprise given that the sheep graze on the indigenous aromatic herbs of Karoo region

▶ **Koeksisters** – the dough is similar of that used for donuts – it is plaited, deep fried and the warm pastry is then dipped in syrup

▶ **Pap and chakalaka** – firm maize porridge similar to polenta served with *chakalaka* a spicy hot sauce made with tomato, onions and peppers

▶ **Perlemoen** – abalone, a seafood delicacy now rarely found on restaurant menus

▶ **Rooibos tea** – refreshing and caffeine free it is produced from the needle fine leaves of an indigenous bush that grows only in the Cederberg

▶ **Samoosas** – small, strongly spiced, triangular shaped pastries, filled with beef or chicken mince or vegetables (photo right)

▶ **Waterblommetjie bredie** – meat or vegetable stew made with indigenous water hyacinth blossoms *(waterblommetjie)* found only in the Cape

CAFÉ ROUX ☺ (U A4) (*Ш a4*)
The Café in leafy Noordhoek serves delicious cakes and fresh salads. A relaxed family spot with a playground for the children and a babysitter for the little ones. Friday is barbecue day. *Tue–Sun 8am–5pm | 270 Chapman's Peak Drive | Noordhoek Farm Village | Noordhoek | tel. 021 7 89 25 38*

CHEF PON'S ASIAN KITCHEN
(129 D6) (*M G6*)

The city's most popular Asian restaurant and you won't get a seat without a reservation. The ambiance is Thai and the authentic Tom Ka Gai chicken coconut soup comes highly recommended. *Daily 6pm–10.30pm | 12 Mill St | Gardens | tel. 021 4 65 58 46*

GANESH (131 F5) (*M N7*)

A small courtyard restaurant serving African cuisine. The kitchen is the focal point in centre and the pots and pans hang on the walls – unconventional and very good value for money. *Mon–Sat from 6pm | corner Lower Main St/Trill St | Observatory | tel. 021 4 48 34 35*

LIMONCELLO (129 D6) (*M G6*)

Small authentic little pizzeria that serves delicious stone fired pizzas. *Mon–Fri noon–3pm, daily 6pm–11pm | 8 Breda St | Gardens | tel. 021 4 61 51 00*

MARCO'S AFRICAN PLACE
(129 D3–4) (*M G4*)

Delicious African culinary delights like ostrich and coconut are on the menu here as is Zulu dancing. The enthusiastic dancers may even encourage you to join in after dessert. Sure to be a fun outing! *Tue–Sat noon–midnight, Sun 3pm–midnight | 15 Rose Lane | Bo-Kaap | tel. 021 4 23 54 12 | www.marcosafricanplace.co.za*

MESOPOTAMIA (129 D4) (*M G4*)

This is South Africa's first Kurdish restaurant and the food here is exotic, hot and spicy. Some nights there are also belly dancers. *Mon–Sat 6pm–1am | corner Long St/Church St | Central | tel. 021 4 24 46 64*

POSTICINO (127 F2) (*M C3*)

A pleasant and affordable alternative to Cape Town's trendy restaurants. The stone

Delicious ostrich steak

fired pizzas are excellent – try their butternut, chilli and bacon signature pizza. *Daily 12.30pm–11pm | 323 Main Rd | Sea Point | tel. 021 4 39 40 14*

ROYALE EATERY (129 D5) (*M F–G5*)

A far cry from your usual fast food joint, the Royale Eatery serves classics with a twist and on weekends this fast food restaurant is always packed with ravenous fans eager for its unusual hamburger creations. *Mon–Sat noon–11pm | 273 Long St | Central | tel. 021 4 22 45 36*

SAIGON (128 C6) (*M F6*)

It is the city's only Vietnamese restaurant and the food is delicious! It has huge windows and the view overlooks the city below. *Daily noon–2.30pm, 6pm–10pm | corner Kloof St/Camp St | Central | tel. 021 4 24 76 69*

YUM (O) (*M G7*)

This is where Capetonians come to relax and enjoy a few quiet hours away from the big city buzz. Try the ravioli with grilled chicken, ham, leeks, sage and mascarpone cheese. *Mon–Thu 4pm–10pm, 11am–10pm, Sat/Sun 9am–10pm | 2 Deer Park Drive | Vredehoek | tel. 021 4 61 76 07*

SHOPPING

WHERE TO START?
Victoria & Alfred Waterfront
(129 D–E 1) (𝑚 G1–2/H2): The V&A Waterfront is Cape Town's shopping paradise. There are several covered car parks but for only ten rand a day there is also the open air car park at the Clock Tower, only a short walk from the main area.

It is easy to shop up a storm in Cape Town, due to the favourable exchange rate, so you may need to buy another bag for all your newly acquired excess luggag.

The city centre has a few good shopping areas: Long Street and Kloof Street are lined with bookstores, wine shops and designer boutiques while St George's Mall – a vibrant and bustling pedestrian zone – is packed with street vendors and stalls that sell everything African arts and crafts to flowers..

In Cape Town your shopping options are endless, there are marketplaces selling flowers and hand-made crafts or areas like the Cape Quarter, in the suburb De Waterkant, that are full of antique shops and elegant furniture stores. If you do decide to browse the shops in the afternoon then you should not dawdle as shops in

Photo: Victoria & Alfred Waterfront shopping precinct

A shoppers' paradise: from wire art to diamond jewellery – Cape Town is a treasure trove full of things for you to take home

central Cape Town close at 5pm on a weekday and as early as 1pm on Saturdays. Shopping malls however stay open late and their trendy boutiques and charming shops are ideal for a shopping excursion. And there is even more to see in the little villages along the False Bay coast, like Simon's Town and Kalk Bay. The latter is full of quaint antique shops and quirky boutiques brimming with clothes, ornaments and art. The prices may not necessarily be that.

ANTIQUES

ANTIQUE ARCADE (129 D4) (*🏛 G4*)
Twelve small shops under one roof: besides furniture there is also plenty of chinaware and delightful bric-a-brac on offer. *127 Long St | Central*

Shopping emporium with over 400 stores: Canal Walk in Milnerton

PRIVATE COLLECTIONS (129 D3) (*ΩΩ G3*)
The shop has the feel of an Indian palace and you will be more inclined to browse than to buy. Private Collection's customers are predominantly interior designers and hotel and restaurant owners whose space can accommodate the imports that range from huge 17th century carved doors to chandeliers and four poster beds. *Mon–Sat 8am–5pm, Sun 9am–2pm | 68 Waterkant St | De Waterkant (Green Point) | www. privatecollections.co.za*

INSIDER TIP THE WHATNOT & CHINA TOWN (U B4) (*ΩΩ b4*)
A melange of antique china, faded postcards of Cape Town, odds and ends and historical black and white Hollywood photos. *Mon–Sat 9am–5pm, Sun 9am–4pm (only until 3pm in winter) | 70 Main Road | Kalk Bay*

BOOKS

BOOK LOUNGE ● (129 E5) (*ΩΩ G5*)
This is the perfect spot to rub shoulders with Cape Town's intellectual crowd. Local authors hold their book launches in the cellar of this well organised and welcoming bookstore. Simply find out what's on, turn up and enjoy some free and wine and snacks. *71 Roeland Street | Central | tel. 021 4 62 24 25 | www.booklounge.co.za*

CLARKE'S ★ (127 D5) (*ΩΩ G5*)
Charming bookstore packed to the rafters with new and old books. A real gem, especially for those who really want to get to grips with South African history and politics. Just about every book that was ever written on the subjects can be found on the shelves here, including the biographies of freedom fighters like Steve Biko and Oliver Tambo. *Mon–Fri 9am–5pm, Sat 9am–1pm | 211 Long St | Central | www. clarkesbooks.co.za*

KALK BAY BOOKS (U B4) (*ΩΩ b4*)
Sink into one of the huge couches and relax with your book of choice. A well organised section on South African authors includes international success stories like J. M. Coetzee and Nadine Gordimer as well as newcomers on the literary scene. *Daily 9am–6pm | 124 Main Rd | Kalk Bay | www.kalkbaybook.co.za*

DELICATESSEN

INSIDER TIP MOUNTAIN VIEW CAFÉ AND TAKEAWAYS (129 D4) (*Ø G4*)

Samoosas are part and parcel of Cape Malay cuisine and this tiny little takeaway sells some of the best in Cape Town. *Daily 7.15am–5.15pm | 171 Long St | Central*

NEWPORT MARKET & DELI (U B2) (*Ø E1*)

The deli stocks a wide selection of local and imported speciality products ranging from cheeses to cold meats. The pastry section has delicious muffins, bagels and artisan breads. Their phrase 'naturally Newport' means that their own products contain no preservatives or additives. *Daily 6.30am– 9pm (winter), in summer until 10pm | 47 Beach Rd | Mouille Point | tel. 021 439 1538*

TORINO (128 B6) (*Ø E5–6*)

This is a must stop for chocoholics and it is conveniently situated on the way up to the Table Mountain cable car base. The owner makes his delicious chocolates on site. Try the truffles or his specialty: chocolate covered orange peel. *34 Kloof Nek Road | Tamboerskloof*

DESIGN

AFRICAN IMAGE (129 D4) (*Ø G4*)

The perfect address if you are looking for an unusual memento to take home with you and a wooden giraffe is not exactly what you had in mind. Instead you will find quirky jewellery, sling bags and other funky items with African motifs, like Mandela clocks. *Corner Church St/Burg St | Central | www.africanimage.co.za*

INSIDER TIP MONTEBELLO DESIGN CENTRE (0) (*Ø M11*)

Situated on an historic site and a short drive from the city centre, this leafy oasis is a design centre where you can watch the craftsmen making the products. See how diamond jewellery is made or the crafting of some very unusual vases. *31 Newlands Avenue | Newlands | www.montebello.co.za*

SHOPPING MALLS

CANAL WALK (U B–C1) (*Ø b–c1*)

Built in a 'Cape Venetian' style on an artificial canal, this massive shopping mall is one of Africa's largest. More than 400 shops, restaurants, a food hall and a cinema complex. *Daily 9am–9pm | Century Blvd | Century City | Milnerton (approx. 20 km/ 12.4mi from the city centre on the N1 in the direction of Paarl) | www.canalwalk.co.za*

CAVENDISH SQUARE (U B2–3) (*Ø b2–3*)

Located just outside of the city in the southern suburbs, this mall is aimed at the youth market with lots of brand names and stores but worth a visit for its unique *Young Designers Emporium* – a success story showcasing the creations of South Africa's young and innovative clothing

---

★ **Clarke's**
Great selection of South African literature → p. 66

★ **Pan African Market**
Cape Town's best market for crafts and musical instruments → p. 69

★ **Green Point Market**
African crafts market at the World Cup Soccer stadium → p. 70

★ **Caroline's Fine Wine Cellar**
For the best selection of local wines → p. 71

MARCO POLO HIGHLIGHTS

designers. They now also have a new branch at the V & A Waterfront. *Mon–Sat 9am–7pm, Sun 10am–5pm | 1 Dreyer St | Claremont | www.cavendish.co.za*

VICTORIA & ALFRED WATERFRONT (129 D–E1) (*M G1–2/H2*)

This harbour shopping precinct plays host to a seemingly endless variety of stores through which some 30 million people make their way every year. From Diesel to Mont Blanc, here you will find a plethora of international brands alongside local fashion chains, department stores, well stocked bookstores and speciality stores that sell anything from cameras to sunglasses. *Musica Megastore* has one of the city's biggest selections of CDs, from kwaito – a music genre that has its origins in hip hop and house – to jazz icons like Hugh Masekela or Abdullah Ibrahim *(Dock Road Complex)*. Added to your shopping experience: live music in the open air auditorium, buskers and traditional dancers and the comings and goings of the tour boats amidst the hustle and bustle of a fully functional harbour! *Daily 9am–9pm | Harbour | www.waterfront.co.za*

WEMBLEY SQUARE (129 E6) (*M G6*)

This is where fashionistas and fitness instructors meet for lunch – of course everybody else does too. This centre in Gardens is where magazines like ELLE are based, as is a popular fitness studio chain. On the ground floor there are trendy cafés, boutiques and designer shops. *Corner Wesley St/Solan Rd | Gardens | www.wembley square.co.za*

GALLERIES

ASSOCIATION FOR VISUAL ARTS (129 D4) (*M G4*)

The exhibition space here rotates well known artists and up-and-coming and emerging talent every three weeks. *35 Church St | Central | www.ava.co.za*

INSIDER TIP BELL-ROBERTS CONTEMPORARY ART GALLERY (130 A3) (*M J5*)

Aside from exhibiting the works of contemporary artists, Brendan and Suzette Bell-Roberts also showcase the publications of their art book publishing house – among them South Africa's leading art magazine 'artsouthafrica'. Scout the neighbourhood for several more galleries. There are new ones springing up all the time and this once run-down suburb is fast becoming the hub of Cape Town's art scene. *Fairweather House | 176 Sir Lowry Rd | Woodstock | www.bell-roberts.com*

BLANK PROJECTS (130 B3) (*M K5*)

This non-profit gallery gives the city's young up-and-coming artists a platform. Find out when they are holding their next opening and go along and get to know the members of the local art scene personally. *Opening times on request | 113–115 Sir Lowry Rd | Woodstock | tel. 072 198 92 21 | www.blankprojects.com*

ERDMANN CONTEMPORARY (129 D4) (*M G4*)

Showcases some of Africa's best photographs. The photographers themselves often pop into the gallery run by owner Heidi Erdmann who is from Namibia. *Mon–Fri 10am–5pm, Sat 11am–2pm | 63 Shortmarket St | Central | tel. 021 4 22 27 62 | www.erdmanncontemporary.co.za*

MICHAEL STEVENSON CONTEMPORARY (130 A3) (*M J5*)

This is arguably the best gallery for contemporary art in Cape Town at the moment. The city's most talented artists are regularly on show here. Michael Stevenson is also actively involved in the art scene in

Pan African Market: for fans of traditional African arts and crafts

Johannesburg, the United States and Europe. *Mon–Fri 9am–5pm, Sat 10am–1pm | 160 Sir Lowry Road | Woodstock | tel. 021 4 62 15 00 | www.stevenson.info*

34 FINE ART (130 A3) (𝄞 J5)

One of Cape Town's leading galleries. Here you will come across works by established South African and international artists. *160 Sir Lowry Rd | Woodstock | www.34long.com*

ARTS & CRAFTS

PAN AFRICAN MARKET ★
(129 D4) (𝄞 G4)

In addition to the huge selection of traditional handcrafted arts and crafts there is also a rather good music shop on the first floor. Profits from the market support more than 200 township families. *76 Long St | Central*

INSIDER TIP STREETWIRES
(129 D4) (𝄞 G4)

From key rings to coffee tables – everything here is handmade from wire and the prices of the items are generally cheaper

than at the V&A Waterfront. *Streetwires* is a community enterprise and all the craftsmen are people who were once previously unemployed. *77/79 Shortmarket St | Central*

MARKETS

INSIDER TIP BAY HARBOUR MARKET
(U A3) (𝄞 a3)

This is still a well kept secret. Stroll through the fashion and food stalls, watch the parade of life go by at the harbour and then relax with a plate of oysters and a glass wine or simply enjoy the seagulls and fishing boats. If you are thinking of taking a bite to eat with you for later on then you should go around to the back of the *Mariner's Wharf* restaurant where you can buy the best tuna in town for your evening *braai. Sat/Sun 10am–5pm, in summer also Fri 4pm–9pm | 31 Harbour Rd | Hout Bay*

CHURCH STREET ANTIQUE MARKET
(129 D4) (𝄞 G4)

You will find this small market, made up of only a few stalls, on Long Street. Handbags from the 1960s, costume jewellery from the 1920s and lots of old coins are amongst the items sold here. *Church St | Central*

FLOWER MARKET (129 E4) (*∅ G4*)
A colourful sea of flowers: for more than a century red roses have been competing with white lilies and indigenous proteas at this inner city market. *Mon–Sat 9am–5pm | Adderley St | Central*

GREEN POINT MARKET ★
(128 C1) (*∅ F2*)
The most popular sport at the Green Point stadium has to be haggling. Be it jewellery,

LOW BUDGET

▶ *Access Park* makes for excellent shopping if you are brand conscious but on a budget: buy Nike, Puma, Guess and plenty of other sports and fashion brands at great prices at this factory outlet on the M5. *Exit Kenilworth, Racecourse* (U B3) (*∅ b3*)

▶ ☺ *Fruit & Veg City* is a very affordable fresh produce chain store ideal for holidaymakers who like to cook their own meals. Locally grown fare ranging from butternut to pawpaw – just about anything you'll need for some of Cape Town's favourite dishes. They will even peel and cut to bite sizes for you! *e.g. corner Kent St/ Drury St | Central* (129 E6) (*∅ H5*).

▶ Ever asked yourself what happens to the design, architecture and fashion magazines that are taken off the shelves to make space for the new? At *Paper Weight* they can be bought at a fraction of their original price *e. g. Canal Walk* (U B–C1) (*∅ b–c1*).

African drums or handcrafted wooden giraffes, whatever you are after, don't give up! You can bargain the item that has caught your eye down to half its original price. *Sun and public holidays 8.30am–6pm | Western Boulevard | Green Point*

MILNERTON FLEA MARKET
(U B1) (*∅ b1*)
Only a 20 minute drive from central Cape Town, this is a collector's dream set against a magical backdrop of Table Mountain and the Atlantic: art deco items, old magazines, antique jewellery and plenty of bric-a-brac looking for a new home. *Sat/Sun 7am–3pm | on the R 27 in the direction of Milnerton*

INSIDER TIP ▶ NEIGHBOURGOODS
MARKET ● ☺ (131 D3) (*∅ M5*)
Eco-friendly is in and Cape Town is no exception! This market (on what used to be industrial land) sells a range of organic products and homemade preserves and condiments, but this is not the only thing that draws Capetonians here on a Saturday. They come here for the lively, street festival atmosphere, the chance to spend the day in the sun enjoying some fresh oysters and a chilled drink. You can also come and shop here during the week. The old mill has been home to a few boutiques and art galleries for a number of years now in a suburb that is gradually emerging from its socially disadvantaged past and growing into the heart of Cape Town's bohemian scene. *Sat 9am–2pm | Old Biscuit Mill | Albert Road | Woodstock*

FASHION

KLÛK & CGDT (128 C2) (*∅ F2*)
Couturiers Malcolm Klûk and Christiaan Gabriel du Toit have become synonymous with the Cape Town design scene. They are known for their unusual creations as

well as their elegant and very wearable everyday fashions. Their designs are still quite affordable despite them being in such demand internationally. *Corner Main Rd/Upper Portswood Rd | Green Point*

JEWELLERY

JEWEL AFRICA
(128 C4) (*771 F4*)
A great place not only to buy jewellery but also to watch over the jewellers shoulder as it is made. Join a free tour that demonstrates how gold chains are produced and diamonds cut. They will also come and collect you from your hotel on request. *Mon–Fri 9am–7.30pm, Sat 9am–5.30pm, Sun 4pm–7pm | tel. 021 4 24 51 41 | 170 Buitengracht St | Central*

OLIVE GREEN CAT
(129 D4) (*771 G4*)
Acrylic is the favourite medium used by jewellery designers Philippa Green and Ida Elsje – be it as a base on which to set a diamond or as a wide bracelet with engraved patterns. Come and feast your eyes on their unusual and unique creations. *76 Church St | Central | www.olive greencat.co.za*

PRINS & PRINS (129 D4) (*771 G4*)
Considered the home of fine jewellery since 1752, Prins & Prins offer exhibition space to various retailers selling gold and silver items of jewellery at relatively affordable prices. You can watch the goldsmiths at work in the cellar. *Corner Hout St/Loop St | Central*

SHOPPING CENTRES

CAPE QUARTER (129 D3) (*771 G3*)
Achieves the perfect balance between commercial hub and charming ambiance! Browse through the galleries and shops then make your way to the brightly coloured central courtyard for a bite to eat at one of many great restaurants. *Mon–Fri 9am–6pm, Sat 9am–4pm, Sun 10am–2pm | The Piazza | 72 Waterkant St | Green Point | www.capequarter.co.za*

Display at Caroline's Fine Wine Cellar

WINE

CAROLINE'S FINE WINE CELLAR ★
(129 D–E4) (*771 G4*)
The selection of superb Cape wines and Cap Classiques – South Africa's answer to champagne – is quite overwhelming. You can also have *Caroline's* ship your purchase home for you. Wine tasting daily. *62 Strand St | Central*

VAUGHAN JOHNSON'S WINE AND CIGAR SHOP (129 D1) (*771 G2*)
Offers expert advice not only when it comes to choosing a fine wine but also the best cigar and when you are making your selection you may well bump into a celebrity doing the same. *Dock Rd | V&A Waterfront*

ENTERTAINMENT

CITY **WHERE TO START?**
Long Street (129 D5–E3)
(🗺 F5–H3): The Focal point of Cape Town's nightlife is Long Street, park in Loop Street (which runs parallel) or Kloof Street, the extension of Long Street's south section. Ask the car guards to find you a spot. Or join the younger crowd in **Observatory's** Lower Main Road with its more alternative nightlife scene. If it's a classy cocktail you are after then try the **Cape Quarter** in De Waterkant.

As soon as the sun has set over the Atlantic Cape Town's nightlife kicks into gear. The bars and clubs in Long Street – the epicentre – open their doors and don't shut them again until the early hours of the morning.

On the promenade in Camps Bay the partygoers carry their Louis Vuitton bags and wear their designer sunglasses – even at ten at night – as they make their way along to the trendy bars and clubs. While over in the student quarter of Observatory the music in the billiard cafés and backpacker bars is turned up so loudly that the whole street gets blasted. Entry to clubs is often free but if there is an admission

Violins and vaudeville: the nights are long in Cape Town and after the concerts and cabarets the bars and clubs open their doors

charge it will usually be between 30 and 40 rand. If a more sophisticated evening, sipping away at a glass of wine, is more up your street then there are plenty of options besides your hotel bar – although the *Daddy Cool Bar* in the *Grand Daddy* hotel comes highly recommended. The chic courtyard of the Cape Quarter in the suburb of De Waterkant is home to a whole array of upmarket bars where you can enjoy an excellent glass of wine or a cocktail. Many locations have a small stage where live music is performed: anything from African jazz to reggae. Culture vultures can indulge in a symphony concert, ballet or theatre production at the *Artscape* theatre complex in the city – it often also stages international musicals. The *Baxter*, a bit further out of the city, also has excellent theatre and comedy productions.

ASOKA SON OF DHARMA
(128 C6) *(⏠ F6)*

This lounge has a really old olive tree in the centre of a lovely courtyard that is surrounded by wooden tables and cosy seating. *Daily 5pm–2am | 68 Kloof St | Gardens | tel. 021 4 22 09 09*

in Cape Town are served here. *Daily noon to 2am | 15 Alfred House | Portswood Road | Waterfront | tel. 021 4 21 03 48 | www.buenavista.co.za*

INSIDER TIP CHENIN WINE BAR
(129 D3) *(⏠ G3)*

At the *Chenin Wine Bar* (previously *The Nose*) in the pleasant Cape Quarter court-

The perfect place to sample some fine wines

BLACK RAM BAR (128 C5) *(⏠ F5)*

A refreshingly unpretentious bar that is a particularly good option on the weekend for a great night out. The *Darling Brew Slow Lager,* brewed just outside of Cape Town, comes highly recommended. Next to the bar is the *Power and Glory*, a fantastic café that is open all day from 8am until 10pm. *Bar Mon–Sat 5pm till late | Kloof Nek, corner Burnside Road | Tamboerskloof | tel. 021 4 22 21 08*

BUENA VISTA SOCIAL CAFÉ
(128 D1–2) *(⏠ F–G2)*

A little bit of Cuba in the middle of Green Point: cigars, mojitos and the best nachos

yard you get to taste your way through a wonderful selection of South African wines as most of the wines can be ordered by the glass. *Daily from 11am | Cape Quarter | De Waterkant | tel. 021 4 25 22 00*

DADDY COOL BAR ★ (129 D4) *(⏠ G4)*

This bar is in the *Grand Daddy* hotel and is a wonderful throwback to the 1980s disco era glitz. It is full of playful décor touches: white leather armchairs, gold coloured wallpaper and mirror ball toilets and it is an ideal place for a glamorous cocktail. *Mon–Tue 4pm–11pm, Fri 4pm–1am, Sat 6pm–1am | Grand Daddy Hotel | 38 Long St | Central | tel. 021 4 24 72 47*

LA MED ★ ☼ (126 A1) (🛍 A7)

Not only can you watch the Lion's Head paragliders come in to land on the stretch of lawn between *La Med's* umbrellas and the ocean, but it is also the perfect spot to watch the sunset as you nurse your sundowner. Turns into a great dance venue at night – especially on Sundays. *Mon–Fri from noon, Sat/Sun from 9am | Victoria Rd | Clifton | tel. 021 4 38 56 00*

INSIDER TIP ▶ PLANET BAR
(128 C5) (🛍 F5)

The *Mount Nelson* bar is as opulent as the hotel itself. Sink into the plush and elegant seats and enjoy your Champagne. *Sat–Thu from 5pm, Fri from 3pm | Mount Nelson | 76 Orange St | Gardens | tel. 021 4 83 17 37*

STONES (131 F5) (🛍 N7)

Billiards bar with loud music and table-soccer games on the first floor. Between games you can always go out onto the balcony to enjoy a cold beer and watch the Lower Main Road's passing parade down below. There is an identical outlet on Long Street. *Daily noon–4am | 84 Lower Main Rd | Observatory | tel. 021 4 48 94 61*

TJING TJING (129 D4) (🛍 G4)

Its stylish roof terrace surrounded by sky-scrapers gives *Tjing Tjing* a New York feel. The architects of the newly opened bar have cleverly combined the elements of the 200 year old building just off Long Street with urban chic. You can order some of the city's best cocktails here. *Daily | 65 Longmarket St | Central | tel. 021 4 22 49 20 | www.tjingtjing.co.za*

CLUBS & DISCOS

BRONX ACTION BAR
(129 D3) (🛍 G3)

Wild bar with dance floor, the hunky waiters are all shirtless and there are a lot of pretty boys swapping telephone numbers. Karaoke on a Monday. *Daily 8pm–2am | corner Somerset Road/Napier St | De Waterkant | tel. 021 4 19 92 16*

CLUB 31 ☼
(129 E4) (🛍 H4)

High up on the 31st floor of a skyscraper in the business district, *Club 31* offers its guests stunning views of the harbour and Table Mountain. There is a dress code so certainly no T-shirts or running shoes. *Thu from 10pm, Fri from 4.30pm, Sat from 10pm | Absa Building | 2 Riebeek St | Central | tel. 021 4 21 05 81 | www.thirtyone. co.za*

DELUXE
(129 D4) (🛍 G4)

A sophisticated retro style club where DJs mix house with traditional African music. Dance the night away and then catch your breath again on the beautiful roof terrace. *Wed, Fri, Sat 10pm–4am | corner Long St/ Longmarket St | Central | tel. 021 4 22 48 32*

★ **Daddy Cool Bar**
Eighties glamour is back at the Grand Daddy Hotel bar on Long Street → p. 74

★ **La Med**
Watch the summer sun slip into the Atlantic with your cocktail in hand → p. 75

★ **Jo'burg**
Partying at its best – and loudest – every night on Long Street → p. 76

★ **Labia**
Cape Town's oldest – and most charming – cinema → p. 77

MARCO POLO HIGHLIGHTS

A good time guaranteed – Mama Africa on Long Street

FICTION (129 D5) (*G5*)

First dance up a storm to hip-hop and electro on *Fiction's* small dance floor, then step outside with a drink and cool off on the balcony overlooking Long Street. *Tue–Sat 9pm–4am | 226 Long St | Central | tel. 021 4 24 57 09*

JO'BURG ★ (129 D5) (*G5*)

This club sets the pace for Cape Town's nightlife, every evening the dance floor is packed with pleasure seekers who stay up until the early hours of the morning dancing the night away to hip-hop, funk, soul and house. *Mon–Sat from noon, Sun from 6pm | 218 Long St | Central | tel. 021 4 22 01 42*

MARVEL (129 D5) (*G5*)

The dance floor here is so small that it only takes three people doing their moves to the hip-hop and electro laid on by the DJs for the place to hot up. At the back, pros wearing their team colours engage in serious table-soccer contests. *Daily 8pm–4pm | 236 Long St | Central | tel. 021 4 26 58 80*

CABARET & COMEDY

ON BROADWAY (129 D3) (*G4*)

Cape Town's only cabaret restaurant offers its audience a fun-filled night of entertainment. The city's drag artists, burlesque dancers and comedy stars will have you in stitches all the way through dinner. *Tue–Sun (also occasionally on Mon) from 6.30pm | 88 Shortmarket St | Central | tel. 021 4 24 11 94*

THEATRE ON THE BAY
(126 A3–4) (*B9*)

You will find this charming little theatre right near the beach in Camps Bay. It belongs to Pieter Toerien, a legend in the South African theatre scene. His sought after productions include adaptations of West End plays or musicals like *Hair*. Regular dance and comedy evenings are also held here. *1 Link St | Camps Bay | tel. 021 4 38 33 00 | www.theatreonthebay. co.za*

CINEMAS

LABIA ★ (128 C5) (*U F5*)
Cape Town's oldest and most charming art-house cinema is in an old theatre that dates back to the 1940s and screens movies you won't find in mainstream cinemas. There is an extra cinema, also belonging to the *Labia,* around the corner at the *Lifestyle Centre (Kloof Street). 68 Orange St | Gardens | tel. 021 4 24 59 27*

VICTORIA & ALFRED WATERFRONT (129 D1–2) (*U G2*)
You can see the latest Hollywood blockbusters in the cinema on the upper level of Victoria Wharf *(tel. 021 4 19 97 00)* while the Cinema Nouveau on the ground floor screens art and foreign language films *(tel. 086 1 30 04 44). Victoria Wharf | V&A Waterfront*

MUSIC

THE ASSEMBLY (129 E55) (*U H5*)
This is rated amongst the city's best live music venues. Originally a warehouse, the industrial interior regularly hosts South African music greats like the *BLK JKS* and *Freshlyground. Opening times vary | 61 Harrington Street | Central | tel. 021 4 65 72 86 | www.theassembly.co.za*

CITY HALL (129 E5) (*U H5*)
The 100 year old city hall is where the Cape Town Symphony and Philharmonic Orchestra is based. The lovely interior with its mosaic floor, stained glass, pipe organ and marble staircase is the perfect backdrop for their Thursday night concerts. With a repertoire ranging from Mozart through to Dvořák, you can get a ticket for as little as 60 rand and sit behind the orchestra. In summer there is the *International Summer Music Festival. Darling St | tel. 021 4 10 98 09 | www.cpo. org.za*

SOCCER OR RUGBY?

▶ Soccer is South Africa's national sport and it is most widely played among the black community. In 2010 it received a special boost when South Africa hosted the Soccer World Cup. Two clubs in Cape Town play Premier Soccer League *(www.psl. co.za)*: Ajax Cape Town and Santos. Athlone Stadium is their home turf but some of their games are held at the Green Point Stadium. Tickets can be bought at the gate on match days. *Athlone | Klipfontein Rd | for more info contact Ajax Cape Town | tel. 021 9 30 60 01*

▶ Rugby has traditionally had its main support base within the white community but things have changed and there are now increasing numbers of players from the black and coloured communities and their inclusion has also meant a far broader support base. The Cape Town team playing in the Super 14 series (alongside other teams from South Africa as well as Australia and New Zealand) are the *Stormers* and their home ground is Newlands Stadium. *Newlands, Boundary Rd | for more info contact Western Province Rugby Union | tel. 021 6 59 45 00 | www. wprugby.com*

MAMA AFRICA (129 D5) (*Ⓜ G5*)
Popular with tourists and locals alike who flock here to enjoy atmosphere and the fantastic African bands, the place is now an institution in Cape Town and they will have you up and dancing in no time. *Mon–Sat from 7pm | 178 Long St | Central | tel. 021 4 26 10 17*

INSIDER TIP MERCURY LIVE AND LOUNGE (129 E6) (*Ⓜ H6*)
Bastion of the indie music scene, on the weekends established rock bands take centre stage on the first floor, while the up-and-coming bands perform in the lounge below where DJs also spin tracks from several pop eras. *Mon–Sat 8pm–*

4am | 43 De Villiers St | Central | tel. 021 4 65 21 06

THE WAITING ROOM (129 D5) (*Ⓜ F5*)
This club on the upper end of Long Street has a genuine party vibe – the age group is 20 to 40. The best DJs play here on the weekend – mostly electronic music – and when you need a breather you can enjoy a beer on the balcony overlooking the hustle and bustle of Long Street. *Mon–Sat 6pm–2am | 273 Long Street | Central | tel. 021 4 22 45 36*

ZULA SOUND BAR (129 D5) (*Ⓜ G5*)
Here DJs take over from popular bands of Cape Town's music scene well into the early hours. Expect to hear mainly electro music and if it gets too loud, go to the balcony and cool off, relax and watch the parade of revellers on Long Street. Every last Wednesday of the month is *Verses* night, an open stage evening for musicians and poets. *Daily from 10am | 194 Long St | Central | tel. 021 4 24 24 42*

LOW BUDGET

▶ Once a week South African comedy star, Kurt Schoonraad, invites colleagues and up-and-coming talent to join him on stage at the *Albert Hall* club. Performers at the *Jou Ma Se Comedy Club* will give you an excellent opportunity to get a feel for how multifaceted the Cape Town sense of humour really can be. *Entrance 70 rand, 35 rand student cardholders | admission from 7.30pm | 208 Albert Rd (130 C3) (Ⓜ L5) | Woodstock | tel. 021 4 47 72 47*

▶ If you feel like spending a quiet evening in your hotel room then stop off at *DVD Nouveau* in the city centre. Indie, art and foreign language, as well as local films all for rent at reasonable prices. Don't forget to take your passport and credit card. *Mon–Sat 10am–8pm, Sun 11am–8pm | 166 Bree St (129 D4) (Ⓜ F–G4) | tel. 021 4 22 49 84*

HIP & TRENDY

CAFÉ CAPRICE (126 A3) (*Ⓜ B9*)
See and be seen – its cool white on white interior is the perfect backdrop for Cape Town's beautiful people to meet and mingle. *Daily from 9am (kitchen closes at 10.30pm) | Victoria Road | Camps Bay | tel. 021 4 38 83 15*

CAFÉ MANHATTAN (129 D3) (*Ⓜ G3*)
A favourite bar in the gay scene. In summer the outside terrace is as packed as the café and house music blares across the entire street. *Daily 10am–2am | 74 Waterkant St | De Waterkant | tel. 021 4 21 66 66*

DIZZY'S (126 A3) (*Ⓜ B9*)
Popular for its karaoke evenings, *Dizzy's* also serves a mean pizza and its relaxed

atmosphere draws a mixed crowd of students, tourists and Cape Town's bon vivants. *In peak season daily 5pm–midnight | 41 The Drive | Camps Bay | tel. 021 4 38 26 86*

ST YVES (126 A3) *(ψ B9)*

Newly revamped, this club on the promenade in Camps Bay is the city's latest hot spot to see and be seen. It has a spacious balcony with expansive views over the beach and the sea and is the favourite hangout for the who's who of Cape Town. When the sun goes down the party really gets going. *Daily | Victoria Road | Camps Bay | tel. 021 4 38 08 26*

TANK (129 D3) *(ψ G3)*

When Hollywood stars visit Cape Town they usually spend some time here so you may catch a glimpse of a few celebrities but the biggest star in *Tank* has to be the massive aquarium that separates the bar from the sushi restaurant. *Daily 12.30pm–3.30pm, 7pm–1am | Cape Quarter | De Waterkant | tel. 021 4 19 00 07*

THEATRE

You can buy tickets for most performances and find out more about what's on at *Computicket*. There is one at the V&A Waterfront, or you can book by phone or online at *www.computicket.com* and pay by credit card *(tel. 083 9158 00)*.

ARTSCAPE (129 F4) *(ψ H4)*

This theatre complex is Cape Town's cultural centre and covers the whole spectrum: opera, symphony concerts, theatre productions and musicals. *DF Malan St | Foreshore | tel. 021 4 10 98 00 | www.art scape.co.za*

BAXTER (U B2) *(ψ b2)*

Comedy and theatre are the kind of productions that are usually performed on the *Baxter's* two stages. You may come across some of the actors hanging out in its restaurant afterwards. *Main Road | Rondebosch | tel. 021 6 85 78 80 | www. baxter.co.za*

Hip and happening – Tank in the Cape Quarter

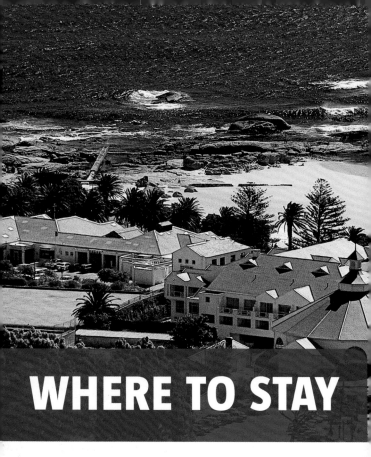

WHERE TO STAY

A play on the Afrikaans name for Cape Town (Kaapstad) 'Slaapstad' means a city that is asleep. This nickname is because everything takes a little longer here than elsewhere thanks to Cape Town's laid back lifestyle. Today it is literally a city that sleeps: the tourism boom of the past few years has meant that Cape Town can sleep just about anyone on any budget.

Accommodation can range from ultra luxurious five-star hotels with sea views and spa facilities, in sought after coastal suburbs like Camps Bay, to backpacker and boutique hotels in the city centre. Many B&B and guest houses – even in the budget price range – are located in beautifully restored old houses and decorated with such flair that you will be forgiven for mistaking them for something out of the glossy pages of an interior design magazine. If a more sophisticated ambience is what you are after you will be more likely to feel at home in Camps Bay or on the Sea Point promenade than in the city centre. The city itself, and its surrounds, also has some attractive options. De Waterkant, Tamboerskloof and Gardens are all picturesque city neighbourhoods with quaint narrow alleyways and delightful cottages. Observatory – characterised by bars, cafés and funky shops – is a university suburb close to the city and a backpackers' haven.

Photo: The Bay Hotel Camps Bay

In Slaapstad you will sleep very well indeed whether it is in a luxury hotel, an elegant villa or a charming backpacker hostel ...

For those on a tight budget there is also the 'backpacker mile' in Long Street and even the option of the more outlying suburbs where you can find some great bargains. If peace and quiet are what you are after then the Constantia Valley – the region's oldest wine growing area – is your best bet, or there is also the tranquil fishing village of Kalk Bay, a good half an hour's drive from central Cape Town.

Prices are generally still quite moderate, especially if you plan your visit in the shoulder season (May to mid September) and are usually negotiable for longer stays. It is also worth looking at the local *Gumtree* website *(capetown.gumtree.co.za)* where many property owners sublet their houses and apartments as holiday rentals. It is a good idea to check them out in person first before you hand over any money!

Winchester Mansions Hotel is conveniently located on the Sea Point promenade

HOTELS: EXPENSIVE

CAMPS BAY RETREAT 🌿
(126 B2) *(𝄞 B8)*

Its rooms and suites incorporate an historical manor house and a modern building. Beautiful waterfalls grace the gardens, alongside them are tennis courts and swimming pools and you also have the mandatory view across the Atlantic and the Twelve Apostles. *15 rooms | 7 Chilworth Rd | Camps Bay | tel. 021 4 37 97 03 | www.campsbayretreat.com*

CAPE HERITAGE HOTEL ⭐
(129 D4) *(𝄞 G4)*

In a building that dates back to 1771, this boutique hotel is centrally located on Heritage Square, which means a whole series of restaurants and bars as well as Long Street are within quick and easy reach on foot. Every room has a style all of its own, be it Moroccan or Malay and there are INSIDER TIP luxurious four-poster beds in four of the rooms. *15 rooms | 90 Bree St | Central | tel. 021 4 24 46 46 | www.cape heritage.co.za*

THE GRAND DADDY **(129 D4)** *(𝄞 G4)*

Housed in a charming Victorian building this hotel is a blend of metropolitan chic and the African art and culture that is the signature of Cape Town's Long Street. In the reception area you will find the works of well known South African artists on display on four plasma screens. The stylishly decorated rooms are remarkably quiet considering its location in the city centre. For a more unusual and perhaps less quiet experience, ask to be booked into one of seven quirkily decorated American airstream trailers on the roof – here you get a hint of a glamorous trailer park holiday with all the amenities that a top hotel can offer. In summer movie classics like 'Dirty Dancing' or 'Breakfast at Tiffany's' are screened on the roof – with popcorn and snacks – and you need not be a guests at the hotel to attend. *26 rooms | 38 Long St | Central | tel. 021 4 24 72 47 | www.granddaddy.co.za*

GREENWAYS HOTEL 😊 **(U B2)** *(𝄞 b2)*

Very centrally located and set in natural surrounds it has a luxurious and environmentally-friendly ambiance with the focus on sustainable energy. *17 rooms | 1 Torquay Avenue | Claremont | tel. 021 7 61 17 92 | www.greenways.co.za*

STEENBERG COUNTRY HOTEL ⭐
(U B3) (*ᗅ b3*)

Nestled beneath the Constantiaberg Mountains, the luxurious Steenberg Estate is a golf course and hotel set amongst rolling vineyards that go on forever. The hotel's beautiful Cape Dutch buildings are some of the Cape's oldest and are listed. The 18-hole golf course is for hotel guests only. *34 rooms | Steenberg Estate | Tokai Rd | Tokai | tel. 021 713 22 22 | www.steenberghotel.com*

VILLA BELMONTE HOTEL ⭐
(O) (*ᗅ F7*)

With only 15 rooms it is the smallest five-star hotel in the region. Some of the classically elegant rooms in the manor house have direct access to the garden at the foot of Table Mountain, the others share a huge terrace with swimming pool and wonderful views over the city. The restaurant serves excellent langoustine, oysters and wine. *15 rooms | 33 Belmont Ave | Oranjezicht | tel. 021 4 62 15 76 | www.villabelmonte hotel.co.za*

THE VINEYARD HOTEL & SPA
(U B2) (*ᗅ b2*)

The stately Vineyard's location is not that central which is why it is slightly more reasonable than other hotels in its class. The building dates back to the end of the 18th century, with a spa and acres of parkland it offers sheer relaxation. *175 rooms | Collington Road | Newlands | tel. 021 6 57 45 00 | www.vineyard.co.za*

WINCHESTER MANSIONS HOTEL
(127 F1) (*ᗅ C2*)

Right on the beach promenade, its colonial ambiance will take you back to the old world charm of the 1920s. Tuesdays is Ladies Night with free cocktails for the ladies and on Sundays there is a live INSIDER TIP Jazz Brunch served in the courtyard. The ● spa programme is complemented by treatment appropriate meals and teas. *76 rooms | 221 Beach Road | Sea Point | tel. 021 4 34 23 51 | www.winchester.co.za*

HOTELS: MODERATE

INSIDER TIP ▶ BERGZICHT
(128 B5) (*ᗅ E5*)

This lovely guest house is renowned for its pleasant service and ideal location in

---

⭐ **Cape Heritage Hotel**
Centrally situated, a superb boutique hotel in an 18th century building → p. 82

⭐ **Steenberg Country Hotel**
For the discerning guest: golf and wine on an historical vineyard estate → p. 83

⭐ **Villa Belmonte Hotel**
Five-star bijou boutique hotel → p. 83

⭐ **iKhaya Lodge**
Where urban comfort meets African charm → p. 85

⭐ **Ashanti Lodge, Guesthouse and Travel Centre**
Comfy, cosy and cheap a pool and palm garden → p. 86

⭐ **Long Street Backpackers**
Come and see why it is Africa's most popular backpacker hostel → p. 87

MARCO POLO HIGHLIGHTS

quiet and leafy Tamboerskloof, right near the city centre. The ☽ pool and garden have a spectacular view of Table Mountain. *8 double rooms, 2 family rooms | 5 Devonport Road | Tamboerskloof | tel. 021 4 23 85 13 | www.bergzichtguesthouse.co.za*

CAPE STANDARD (128 B2) (*ⅅ E2*)

Small but inviting with an interior filled with design classics by Mies van der Rohe and an exterior with a sun deck with loungers by the pool. INSIDER TIP Rooms No. 8 and 9 have sea views. *9 rooms | 3 Romney Road | Green Point | tel. 021 4 30 30 60 | www.capestandard.co.za*

CAPE VICTORIA GUESTHOUSE (128 B2) (*ⅅ E2*)

Its charming owner Lily has been spoiling her guests at this family run establishment for the past 15 years. Her great taste in antiques turns each room into a stylish but comfortable refuge. It also has a swimming pool. *10 rooms | 13 Torbay Road | Green Point | tel. 021 4 39 77 21 | www.cape victoria.co.za*

DADDY LONG LEGS (129 D4) (*ⅅ G4*)

A fashionable hotel on Long Street ideal for those who want to stay in the thick of things without having to do the backpacker thing

LUXURY HOTELS

The Bay Hotel Camps Bay ☽ (126 A–B3) (*ⅅ B9*)

Pristine white hotel in a prime location in the middle of trendy Camps Bay. Most rooms have stunning views of Cape Town's best beach stretching out right in front of the hotel. Added attraction for its well-heeled guests is the lovely pool area – a great alternative when the beach gets busy. *72 rooms, 6 suites | approx. 2500–6500 rand | 69 Victoria Rd | tel. 021 4 37 97 01 | www.thebay.co.za*

Cape Grace ☽ (129 D2) (*ⅅ G2*)

This exclusive hotel on the V&A Waterfront has its own quay and marina and is surrounded by water on three sides. All the rooms have spectacular views either of the harbour or Table Mountain. The bright décor and specialised relaxation treatments in the ● spa facility are typically African. *122 rooms | 5000–13,000 rand | West Quay | V&A Waterfront | tel. 021 4 10 71 00 | www.capegrace.com*

Mount Nelson (128 C5) (*ⅅ F5*)

The distinctive pale pink exterior of the 'Nelly' (as Capetonians fondly call it) marks it as the city's most exclusive hotel. In a class all of its own it always makes it to the top of international hotel rankings and is often the choice of celebrities and Hollywood stars. The ● *Librisa Spa* is a true treat – the children are looked after while you relax. *201 rooms | from 5000 rand | 76 Orange St | Central | tel. 021 4 83 10 00 | www.mountnelson.co.za*

Twelve Apostles Hotel and Spa ☽ (126 A6) (*ⅅ A11*)

Nestled below the foot of the Twelve Apostles mountain range this hotel, hewn into the sandstone rock face, not only offers its guest a luxurious stay but also a spa, two swimming pools, a cinema and magnificent and sweeping views of the Atlantic. *70 rooms | 5000–15,000 rand | Victoria Road | Camps Bay | tel. 021 4 37 90 00 | www.12apostleshotel.com*

Sophisticated luxury – elegant suites at the Mount Nelson Hotel

or fit in with the posh guests at the *Grand Daddy*. All the rooms have a character all of their own and some are similar to stylish self-catering apartments. *13 rooms, 6 apartments | 134 Long St | Central | tel. 021 4 22 30 74 | www.daddylonglegs.co.za*

IKHAYA LODGE ★
(129 D6) (*M G6*)

iKhaya is Xhosa for 'at home' and its eclectic mix of urban comfort and African flair will have you feeling like that in no time. Right on your doorstep are the cafés of charming Dunkley Square while the city centre and Gardens are within easy walking distance. *11 rooms, 2 suites, 8 apartments | Dunkley Square/Wandel St | Gardens | tel. 021 4 61 88 80 | www.ikhayalodge.co.za*

NINE FLOWERS (128 D6) (*M F–G6*)

Every room in this guest house is dedicated to a flower and a number of interior design magazines have already featured its interiors. Hosts Matthias and Marrin also offer day trips. Beautiful location next to the Company's Gardens. *8 rooms | 133–135 Hatfield St | Gardens | tel. 021 4 62 14 30 | www.nineflowers.com*

ROMNEY LODGE (128 B2) (*M E2*)

Mediterranean flair combined with African colonial décor and an outdoor area with a secluded deck terrace and swimming pool. *6 rooms | Romney Rd | Green Point | tel. 021 4 34 48 51 | www.romneylodge.co.za*

THE WALDEN HOUSE (128 B5) (*M E5*)

This Victorian building has beautiful interiors done in an elegant colonial style. White cotton bedding, ceiling fans, mosquito nets and white floorboards all add to the atmosphere. Four of the rooms have direct access to the garden with pool. *6 rooms, 1 suite | 5 Burnside Road | Tamboerskloof | tel. 021 4 24 42 56 | www.walden-house.com*

WELGELEGEN GUESTHOUSE
(128 C6) (*M F6*)

A boutique hotel with rooms stylishly decorated by its interior design owner. The accommodation is in two Victorian buildings with a romantic courtyard with pool. Only a stone's throw away from the bars, cafés and shops of Kloof Street and the city centre. Also with an in house treatment room for pampering. *13 rooms, 1 apart-*

Good value – Long Street Backpackers

ment | 6 Stephen St | Gardens | tel. 021 4 26 23 73 | www.welgelegen.co.za

WHALE COTTAGE GUESTHOUSE
(126 B4) (B10)

The name speaks for itself and if you happen to stay there at the right time, you will be able to whale and dolphin watch from the terrace. Its position in the heart of stylish Camps Bay means that the beach-front is only steps away. *10 rooms | 57 Camps Bay Drive | Camps Bay | tel. 021 4 33 21 00 | www.whalecottage.com*

HOTELS: BUDGET

ALOE HOUSE (131 E4) (*N6*)

Small lovingly restored B&B in Observatory with neat and functional rooms with spacious showers fitted with black slate tiles. Excellent value for money. *2 rooms | 12 Howe St | tel. 021 4 48 53 37 | www.aloe house.co.za*

ASHANTI LODGE AND TRAVEL CENTRE
★ (128 C6) (*F6*)

This upmarket backpacker and guest house is located in a lovely Victorian house with pool, sundeck and a great view of Table Mountain from the café on the first floor. Twelve double rooms and ten dormitories with six to eight beds in the lodge, another seven double rooms with communal kitchen in the second building around the corner. *11 Hof St | Gardens | tel. 021 4 23 87 21 | www.ashanti.co.za*

BAYVIEW LODGE (U A3) (*a3*)

A peaceful haven that is a short 20 minute drive from the city centre and at affordable prices. The seven rooms and the self-catering apartment have been beautifully decorated, the atmosphere is homely. The views of Hout Bay harbour and the valley from the patio are a treat, as is the salt water swimming pool. *19 Luisa Way | Hout Bay | tel. 021 7 90 68 68 | www. bvlodge.co.za*

CACTUSBERRY LODGE 🌿 (O) (*G6*)

Artistically decorated guest house with amazing view of Table Mountain. For breakfast try their INSIDERTIP special Moroccan bread. *6 rooms | 30 Breda St | Vredehoek | tel. 021 4 61 97 87 | www. cactusberrylodge.com*

ELEPHANT'S EYE LODGE ☺
(U B3) (🗺 b3)

Run on solar energy, this quiet family friendly B&B is a short 30 minute drive from central Cape Town. It is a pleasant Cape Dutch farmhouse in the Constantia Valley near the Tokai Forest. *6 rooms | 9 Sunwood Drive | Tokai | tel. 021 7 15 24 32 | www.elephantseyelodge.co.za*

THE STABLES
(U B3) (🗺 b3)

The rooms in this guest house, in the Constantia Valley, are in converted stables. They all have their own patio plus there is a huge garden with swimming pool, they also serve a lavish six-course breakfast. *7 rooms | Chantecler Lane | Constantia | tel. 021 7 94 36 53 | tstables@mweb.co.za*

17 ON LOADER (129 D3) (🗺 G3)

Stylish guest house in the picturesque De Waterkant. You have a magnificent view of the whole city from the ☼ roof terrace. There is also the option of a self-catering cottage. *11 rooms, 3 cottages | 17 Loader St | De Waterkant | tel. 021 4 18 34 17 | www.17loader.za.net*

BACKPACKERS

THE GREEN ELEPHANT
(131 E5) (🗺 N6)

Guests who book into this hostel, in the student quarter of Observatory, are in for a welcome surprise. Its creature comforts include: a solar heated pool, whirlpool, television set and internet access. You can even camp in the garden. *4 dormitories and 9 rooms | 57 Milton Rd | tel. 021 4 48 63 59 | www.hostels.co.za*

LONG STREET BACKPACKERS ★
(129 D5) (🗺 G5)

With a 'Hoscar' – the award for the continent's best hostel – to its name, service, comfort and prices here are right on par! Not noisy at night despite its location right in the middle of the city's nightlife. Sunday is free stew day. *16 dormitories, 15 rooms | 209 Long St | Central | tel. 021 4 23 06 15 | www.longstreetbackpackers. co.za*

33 SOUTH BOUTIQUE BACKPACKERS
(131 F5) (🗺 N7)

The perfect spot for the young and adventurous to start their holiday slightly off the usual tourist track. The team in charge is as relaxed as the student district itself and always have some good tips on what is on in Obz – be it a party or cultural event. *48 Trill Rd | Observatory | tel. 021 4 47 24 23 | www.33southbackpackers.com*

LOW BUDGET

▶ *Cape Town Backpackers* is a comfortable and conveniently located hostel with Long Street and Kloof Street not far off. The rooms are simple but offer real value for money. There are extra rooms in a small house behind it with their own balcony. *5 dormitories, 16 rooms | 81 New Church St* **(128 C5) (🗺 F5)** *| tel. 021 4 26 02 00*

▶ Cheap and unusual: sleep in a converted train cabin on the *African Train Lodge* parked behind the railway station. Extra facilities like a television room, pool table and kitchen are in a converted passenger waiting room by the railway track. There is of course a dining carriage and even a swimming pool. *56 rooms | Monument Station | Old Marine Dr | Central* **(129 F5)** *(🗺 J5) | tel. 021 4 18 48 90 | www. trainlodge.co.za*

WALKING TOURS

The tours are marked in green in the street atlas, the pull-out map and on the back cover

① THE GARDENS AND THE HISTORY OF THE CITY CENTRE

The history of the suburb of Gardens goes back to 1652 when the city's first park was opened to members of the public. Some of Cape Town's most important cultural and architectural buildings are located here. Route: approx. 2km/1.2mi, duration around one hour.

Begin your walking tour at Bertram House on Government Avenue by the Company's Gardens. This red face brick museum is one of Cape Town's last remaining Georgian buildings. It houses a vast and varied col-lection – from English jewellery to Chinese porcelain. A few steps away are some of the city's most interesting cultural sites. The pristine white building of the South African National Gallery → p. 32 – founded back in 1872 with art exhibits from the 17th century onwards. Today its temporary exhibitions are its pièces de résistance. In Hatfield Road just behind it is the Jewish Museum → p. 29 housed in a former synagogue. It is a good idea to do this walk with a tour guide to get a true picture of how steeped in history this part of Cape Town really is. In the Company's Gardens → p. 29 is a large statue of colonial pioneer Cecil John Rhodes

Up close and personal: get a real feel for this metropolis as you make your way through its diverse neighbourhoods on foot

who founded the De Beers diamond conglomerate in the 19th century and Rhodesia (today Zimbabwe) bordering South Africa. Flanking the gardens are the imposing neoclassical Houses of Parliament → p. 30. You can take a guided tour of the interior and if you are in luck you may catch parliament in session. Outside, the statue of former South African Prime Minister Jan Smuts is right near that of

Queen Victoria, epitomising the city's British heritage. Another distinctly British presence is St George's Cathedral → p. 36 the seat of the Anglican Church in Cape Town, with its impressive stained glass windows.

For Capetonians walking through the Company's Gardens at the end of a working day or simply taking a leisurely stroll, this beautiful park has become part and

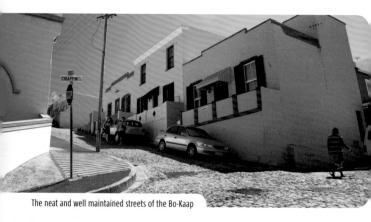

The neat and well maintained streets of the Bo-Kaap

parcel of everyday life. So much so that they are almost impervious to the history that permeates the heart of their city and see it simply as a lovely place to enjoy their lunch hour or to have a quick chat with friends. Amble through it and enjoy its past, relax on a park bench under the magnificent old trees with a snack and rest your weary feet! Keep in mind that a no alcohol policy applies to public places.

As the sun begins to set, leave the gardens and take Wale Street down to the cobbled stretch of Church Street. This tree-lined pedestrian precinct is always buzzing with life and the area is filled with street cafés, art galleries, antique dealers and market stalls that hold the promise of a bargain! Aside from all the items for sale the people who frequent this vibrant area make for some fascinating people watching.

Next you should move on to Long Street → p. 30, the liveliest of Cape Town's streets. This is where the nightlife is focused and its quaint Victorian buildings are home to many restaurants and clubs – most with balconies from which you can watch it all unfold before you. For a quieter evening, head further up the street until you reach Kloof Street → p. 30 where the restaurants and atmosphere is a lot calm-er. Here you can do as Capetonians do, wine, dine and discuss and – most importantly of all – relax and enjoy!

② THE BO-KAAP – STEP BACK IN TIME TO ANOTHER WORLD

Every day on the dot at midday the noon gun is fired from Signal Hill and nowhere does the sound carry as loudly as through the small cobbled alleyways of the Bo-Kaap – the colourful Malay district beneath it. The residents here, mainly Capetonians of Asian descent, don't even flinch. The daily ritual goes back to 1806 and was once used as a time signal for ships anchored in Table Bay. Route: approx. 2.8km/1.7mi, duration around 1.5 hours.

The walk starts at *Marco's African Place (15 Rose Lane)* – it is usually possible to find parking in the side streets nearby – from where you will step into one of the city's few historic neighbourhoods. Make your way up Rose Street to admire the colourfully painted houses. Its residents may not necessarily be well-to-do, but they take great pride in the upkeep of their homes, some of which are over a hundred years old and are listed. Don't forget to take your camera as the afternoon light, picturesque cobbled alleyways and unique architecture all make for an ideal photo opportunity. Do be circumspect when taking pictures and ask nicely if you think you are imposing!

Typically you will see children on rollerblades, women lugging home their shopping, pensioners sitting outside on their patios watching the comings and goings on the cobbled streets and a few other tourists strolling around just like yourself. When the hour is right, you will hear the mosque crier call his congregation to prayer across the rooftops. Many families have been living here for generations. More recently the creative urban youth have also moved in. There are the occasional social issues that arise, but all in all, the suburb is on an even keel and welcomes visitors.

Carry on walking for a few minutes until you reach Wale Street. Across the road is the **Bo-Kaap Museum** (71 Wale Street) with small but very worthwhile exhibits about this interesting suburb. When you are done simply turn right into Wale Street then right again into Chiappini Street. The home owners here must be particularly good customers of Cape Town's paint shops as it seems as though their homes have been painted with the perfect colour sequence in mind: green, purple, blue and yellow facades one after the other. Amble along the side streets and buy a few sweet pastries in the neighbourhood's local stores. In the mood to test your fitness levels? Then walk all the way to the top of Longmarket Street, which feels on foot as if it is the world's steepest road! An older car will probably give up on you up the slope, but if you can get to the top on foot you can be sure that it will be well worth the effort. Once at the top you will see the magnificent panorama of Cape Town that unfolds across the rooftops of the Bo-Kaap.

As sunset slowly approaches it is a good idea to head back down via Chiappini Street, keep left and follow Castle Street and you will soon be back to where you started out. Before you go back though, an absolute must is a detour to the **Cape Quarter**, one of Cape Town's most stylish shopping centres with fabulous cafés and all kinds of delightful small shops.

 ## OBSERVATORY – BOHEMIAN AND UNPRETENTIOUS

Observatory is not really regarded as a tourist attraction which is not such a bad thing because it means that this student quarter has retained its funky, down to earth charm. The suburb is actually one of Cape Town's most interesting. Even in the final years of apartheid people of all races managed to defy the government and live here together despite the Group Areas Act which decreed that each population group had to live in their own designated area. Integration was against the law. The area was, until quite recently, a bit dodgy but it has undergone a revival and today you can safely visit at anytime during the day or night. Route: approx. 3.5km/2.1mi, duration around 2 hours.

Start your walk on the Main Road on to Lower Main Road which will take you into the vibrant heart of Observatory → p. 43. None of its other side streets have quite the same allure as Lower Main Road with its profusion of little cafés, galleries and quirky shops like e.g. *Revolution Records* with its selection of 20,000 records. Next door is a distinctly African pub, nothing more than a billiard table, television set and a bar counter – possibly with a few beer drinking students – and not a tourist in sight. The smell of burning incense wafting across the road will be from *Kilimanjaro,* luring shoppers in to admire the shop's crystals and African garments. A few doors on is **INSIDER TIP** Mimi's *(107 Lower Main Road)*, a corner café and deli with a charm all of its own. Its tiny shabby chic interior has white wooden chairs with the varnish peeling off them and great organic fare. There are only a few tables outside and if you decide to lunch here, try the quiche and a delectable smoothie. The windows are usually full of posters so you can check out the upcoming events in Observatory – anything from small concerts to book readings. Some of which take place right next door in the legendary *Obz Café* and *Theatre*. It may be a bit early in the day for a live show so stroll across to the other side of the street where you will find *Obz Books*, a dusty gem of a bookstore stuffed with thousands of books stacked all over its shelves, it is an excellent source for non-fiction books about South African politics in the 1960s and 1970s – a shop that breathes history!

The social heart of Obz is the Lower Main Road but you may want to wander through some of the side streets to see what else there is. Stop to watch the local children playing in the playgrounds, take a peek into an African hair salon or go inside one of the quaint old churches. It will soon become very obvious that this suburb is far off the beaten tourist track. Obz is a slice of everyday South African life, sometimes a little improvised but always friendly. Find your way back to Lower Main Road and stroll further down, past the antique shops and ● **art galleries**. Look out for *These Four Walls (168 Lower Main Rd)* or *Urban Contemporary Art Gallery (46 Lower Main Rd)* – the owners will gladly take you around their latest exhibits. If you are feeling a little peckish then try the *Respella Crêperie* – right next to yet another shop with incense wafting from it.

After a while it becomes obvious that not all the buildings in Observatory have been restored and that the area is still in the throes of change. Some houses are in a state of total disrepair. Once again keep in mind that as a rule in South Africa it is always best not to set out alone and

Old Biscuit Mill Market – where everybody meets to relax

carry as little money or as few valuables as possible on your person. Saturdays in Obz are probably your best option because then you can also pop in at the Old Biscuit Mill Market only 20 minutes away. To get there, at the end of Lower Main Road turn left into Albert Road. The quaint boutiques and shops suddenly disappear and make way for a typically African shopping street with plenty of rather chaotic shops selling all kinds of junk – and some interesting antiques or keepsakes – you would not find elsewhere. Keep walking on this street for about 20 minutes until you come to the INSIDER TIP Old Biscuit Mill Market. It is easy to spot because hundreds of local tourists and hip arty folk throng here for the afternoon.

4 BEACHFRONT PROMENADE – LIFE IS A BEACH

It is hard to believe that in the early 1990s all you would see here were some rundown harbour warehouses and a few dubious pubs. Today the Victoria & Alfred Waterfront is one of the continent's most expensive tracts of real estate. There is no other South African site that attracts as many tourists and it is quite easy to blow your entire travel budget in its upmarket stores. Far easier on your pocket: set out from here on a nice long walk. Route: 8km/5mi, duration around 3 hours.

Start your walk by putting your wallet (and the shops) out of your mind and taking a stroll through the area. You will have Table Mountain in all its glory as a backdrop and the hustle and bustle of the harbour in front of you. This is where the tourist boats and private yachts set off from, as does the ferry to Robben Island → p. 40. The massive commercial harbour next door is largely out of view from here but always in full swing.

Buskers are part and parcel of the Waterfront so you will usually be able to pause along the way to enjoy the sounds of a marimba band or watch traditional dancers gyrating to a rhythmic drum beat. Then head off to ● Green Point Stadium. It is here where soccer icon Diego Maradona broke down in tears in 2010 when his Argentinean team was knocked out in the quarter finals. There are stadium tours several times a day so you can explore the terrain where your favourite team once played their deciding match *(90 minutes – just like a football match | approx. 60 rand)*. Find out more at the stadium's visitor centre which is well signposted. The entire area used to be a golf course but the massive stadium (it can seat 65,000 spectators) is now surrounded by a beautifully landscaped park with attractive gardens and playgrounds.

Now stroll along the beach promenade – but only as far as your feet will carry you – this is one of the longest promenades in any international city, measuring 6km/3.7mi. If not the longest then it is definitely one of the most spectacular! Don't get caught off guard though, the intensity of the waves crashing against the promenade can quite easily leave you completely soaked in seconds. The promenade is a meeting place for the whole spectrum of Cape Town residents. From the young to the old, the folk simply out for a stroll, the slightly unfit to the improbably beautiful, the joggers and the rollerbladers – all Cape Town can be found out and about on this walkway. Children play ball on the lawns, families picnic and everyone people watches. If you still have some energy left then now is the time for a swim at the Sea Point Pavilion → p. 45 swimming pool. On your way back you should drop in at *Giovanni's Café Bar (103 Main Rd | Green Point)* for one of their famous ham sandwiches.

TRAVEL WITH KIDS

CAPE POINT OSTRICH FARM
(U B5) (🗺 b5)

How much does an ostrich egg weigh? How long does it takes to hatch? Learn all the facts at the only ostrich farm on the Cape peninsula. There is also a restaurant on site. *Daily 9.30am–5.30pm | tours 40 rand children | tel. 021 7 80 92 94 | Plateau Rd | just north of the entrance to the Cape of Good Hope Table Mountain National Park*

CAVE GOLF ● (129 D1) (🗺 G2)

You hoped to take your family for a round of golf but the rain put a damper on your plans? Not a problem as there is always *Cave Golf* at the V&A Waterfront. The 18 holes of this mini golf course are deceptively difficult, but should guarantee fun for the whole family. *Daily 9am–5pm | V&A Waterfront | tel. 021 4 19 94 29*

PLANETARIUM
(128–129 C–D5) (🗺 F–G5)

Star watching before dark? Visit the planetarium and you get to see the night sky over Cape Town – throughout the day. The planetarium forms part of the *South African Museum*. Find out what shows are on before you go: some are perfect for small children while others more suited to amateur astronomers and youngsters in their late teens. *Daily 10am–5pm | shows 25 rand, 10 rand children | tel. 021 4 81 39 00 | South African Museum | 25 Queen Victoria St | Company's Gardens*

PUTT PUTT COURSE (128 A1) (🗺 D–E2)
Popular mini golf course near Mouille Point promenade. *Daily 9am–9pm | 14 rand | Bill Peters Drive | Mouille Point | tel. 021 4 34 68 05*

RATANGA JUNCTION (U B–C1) (🗺 b–c1)
A large amusement park with wild roller coaster rides ideal for thrill seeking children. For the younger ones there are always the merry-go-rounds and boat rides. *Only in summer, daily 10am–5pm | Century City Boulevard | Century City | Milnerton | 142 rand (1.30 m/4ft tall and above), 70 rand (under 1.30 m/4ft)*

SAFARIS
Even if they are not your typical 'Out of Africa' experience, these two game reserves are relatively close proximity to

Learn about the night sky or go on a safari: some educational, exciting and creative activities for children

Cape Town are well worth a visit. They have the big five, game rides and four-star accommodation: *Aquila Safari (www.aquila safari.com | tel. 021 4 31 84 00)* and *Inverdoorn Game Reserve (Ceres | www.inver doorn.com | tel. 021 4 34 46 39)*.

SCRATCH PATCH (129 D1) (ₘ G2)
Trays filled with thousands of semi precious polished gemstones (like rose quartz and lapis lazuli) where children can 'scratch' for their favourites. The bags they fill are weighed and priced accordingly. They also have a branch in Simon's Town where you can see the stones being processed (U B5) (ₘ b5). *Daily 9am–sunset | Dock Rd | V&A Waterfront | tel. 021 4 19 94 29 | www.scratchpatch.co.za.*

INSIDER TIP ▸ SERENDIPITY MAZE
(128 A1) (ₘ D1–2)
If you find your way to the centre then your wish will be granted but first you have to find your way through the labyrinth. *Serendipity Maze* is the third largest maze in the world and Jonathan Durr, the man who runs it, looks just like a character straight out of a storybook. *Mon–Fri 2pm–7pm, Sat/Sun 10am–7pm | 20 rand, 15 rand children | Beach Rd | Mouille Point | tel. 076 9 03 11 02*

WORLD OF BIRDS (U A3) (ₘ a3)
World of Birds is Africa's largest aviary with more than 3000 birds and you can walk through it on pathways that are covered over in wire. But there are not only birds, a special treat is the *Monkey Jungle* where your children can make friends with the small, inquisitive and tame squirrel monkeys. About a 30 minute drive from the city. *Daily 9am–5pm | 75 rand, 40 rand children | Valley Rd | Hout Bay | www.world ofbirds.org.za*

GARDEN ROUTE

When European settlers first arrived on this section of the South African coast they found an abundance of lush vegetation – the entire coastal stretch along the Indian Ocean is covered in wild natural forests and delicate and colourful fynbos. It looked like an exuberant garden – hence the name Garden Route.

From Mossel Bay to the Tsitsikamma National Park further north, the overwhelming beauty of this entire coastal stretch (that covers about 200 km/124mi) will unfold before you: isolated beaches and bays, cliffs covered in jungle-like overgrowth and deep ravines that carve their way through to the sea. The rivers that course through the ravines here are so dark that they almost look black as their waters are infused with tannins from the rich forest soil. When they flow into the sea their dark waters swirl together with the beautiful blue of the warm Indian Ocean. The solitude of the countryside is contrasted with the hustle and bustle of the charming little coastal villages, one of which, *Knysna,* is the unofficial capital of the Garden Route. It is regularly voted South Africa's top holiday destination and makes an ideal base from which to explore the region's highlights. The distances for day trips from here are very manageable but there are many other

Photo: Suspension bridge in the Tsitsikamma National Park

Unspoilt forests and black water rivers, secluded beaches, untouched wilderness and sleepy coastal towns along the warm Indian Ocean

(often cheaper) options to stay all along the coast.

On your trip to, or from, Cape Town, it is a good idea to take the R 62 through the semi-desert of the Klein Karoo, in the Eastern Cape's hinterland, and to plan for up to two overnight stays. The stark contrast between this barren landscape and the lush coastal region is quite remarkable. A stop at *Oudtshoorn* – the international capital of ostrich farming – is mandatory but the superlatives this region is known for do not end here. The R 62 is also the world's longest wine route with the austere climate conditions making the region ideal for port, brandy and dessert wines, so be sure to stop along the way to take in some wine tasting. *Calitzdorp*, some 50 km/31mi from Oudtshoorn, is South Africa's undisputed port wine capital. Best to set aside a whole week for the Garden Route so you get to see it in its full multifaceted glory. The following towns are not listed alphabetically but sequentially, as you come up from Cape Town.

Replica sailing ship in the Bartolomeu Dias Museum

MOSSEL BAY

(133 E6) (*X18*) **From 1500 onwards Portuguese seafarers replenished their supplies here and would exchange news by leaving messages in an old milkwood tree.**
The tree in this coastal town then went on to become famous as South Africa's first post office. Mossel Bay (population of 35,000), named after the abundance

of mussels by the Dutch in the 17th century, is today a vibrant harbour and holiday resort town.

BARTOLOMEU DIAS MUSEUM COMPLEX
Named after the European seafarer who first dropped anchor in South Africa in 1488, this museum covers local history and is also where you will find the *Post Office Tree* – you can still send a letter from here today. *Mon–Fri 9am–4.45pm, Sat/Sun 9am–3.45pm | 1 Market St | www.diasmuseum.co.za*

Beckoning you just below the town is *Santos Beach*, a lovely swimming beach on the warm Indian Ocean.

BAY LODGE ON THE BEACH
The name says it all and what better way to fall asleep than to the sound of the waves. *9 rooms | 29 Bob Bower Crescent | tel. 044 6 95 06 90 | www.bay-lodge.co.za | Moderate*

MOSSEL BAY TOURISM BUREAU
Corner Market St/Church St | tel. 044 6 91 22 02 | www.visitmosselbay.co.za

GEORGE

(133 E5–6) (*X17–18*) **The small town founded in 1811 (pop. 105,000) lies between the imposing Outeniqua Mountains and the warm Indian Ocean and is the Garden Route's commercial hub.**

Its internationally acclaimed *Fancourt* golf estate makes it a magnet for golf enthusiasts. Among some of the famous tournaments held here are the President's Cup, in honour of Nelson Mandela, and the first women's world cup championship.

SIGHTSEEING

OLD SLAVE TREE
Distinctive for the old iron chain that has grown into its trunk – this 200 year old oak tree is where slave auctions were once held and is now a national monument. *York Street*

THE OUTENIQUA CHOO-TJOE ★
Twice daily (except Sun) this historical train steams its way through stunning scenery on a two hour return trip between the towns of George and Mossel Bay. The future of the train ride hangs in the balance as the original stretch between George and Knysna is closed (at the time of going to press) due to flood damage. Book your tickets in George: *tel. 044 8 01 82 88 | return trip 100 rand*

SPORTS & ACTIVITIES

FANCOURT
This golf resort ranks among the finest courses in the world due in part to the magnificent design of the 18-hole green by South African golfing great Gary Player, combined with the exclusivity of its luxury hotel in its magnificent setting. Green fees for non-members from 380 rand. *Montagu St | tel. 044 8 04 00 30 | www.fancourt.com*

INFORMATION

GEORGE TOURISM BUREAU
124 York St | tel. 044 8 01 92 95 | www.tourismgeorge.co.za

WHERE TO GO

OUDTSHOORN ★ (133 E5) (*Ø X17*)
You reach Oudtshoorn, which is about 50 km/31mi from George, via the impressive ✄ *Outeniqua Pass*. This town is the most important in the semi-desert Klein Karoo and is the world's most successful ostrich farming region. A visit to one of the farms is certainly worthwhile and *Highgate Ostrich Show Farm* is the world's oldest ostrich farm *(tel. 044 2 72 71 15 | approx. 10 km/6.2mi outside Oudtshoorn in the direction of Mossel Bay, follow signage on the R 328)*. Oudtshoorn's *Jemima's* is one of South Africa's top ten restaurants and you should try the INSIDER TIP Karoo lamb prepared with regional spices. Reservations essential! *(Tue–Sun 11am–2pm, 6pm–10pm | 94 Baron van Reede St | tel. 044 2 72 08 08 | Moderate)*. Stay over at *Foster's Manor*, a former ostrich farm *(8 rooms | 52 Voor-*

★ **The Outeniqua Choo-Tjoe**
A scenic ride through nature on an old steam train
→ p. 99

★ **Oudtshoorn**
Ostrich farm capital of the world → p. 99

★ **Featherbed Nature Reserve**
Nature reserve right on the lagoon → p. 100

★ **Tsitsikamma National Park**
Marine coastal reserve ideal for scenic hikes and overnights → p. 103

MARCO POLO HIGHLIGHTS

trekker Rd | tel. 044 2 79 26 77 | Budget–Moderate).
Information: *Oudtshoorn Tourism Bureau | Baron van Reede St | tel. 044 2 79 25 32 | www.oudtshoorninfo.com*

WILDERNESS NATIONAL PARK
(133 E5–6) *(ⓜ X17–18)*
Some 18 km/11mi from George, this national park stretches along the coast for 28 km/17.3mi. It has a remarkable diversity of flora and fauna thanks to an ecosystem formed with the merging of the Indian Ocean with freshwater mountain rivers. It is an area of exceptional beauty that is also ideal for abseiling, cycling and canoeing. Enquire at the *Wilderness Tourism Bureau (Leila's Lane | tel. 044 8 77 00 45 | www.tourismwilderness.co.za)*. The park offers overnight log cabins, huts (*Budget*) and camping facilities. *Ebb & Flow Camp signposted on the N 2 east of the town of Wilderness | tel. 044 8 77 11 97 | www.sanparks.org*

KNYSNA

(133 E6) *(ⓜ X18)* **South Africans regularly vote Knysna (population of 30,000) as their favourite holiday resort and the town is so well geared for tourists.**

With an influx of around two million tourists a year its appeal is no secret and the Waterfront with its many restaurants and souvenir shops is where it all happens. Running through town is the Knysna Lagoon that has at its estuary the *Featherbed Nature Reserve* which can only be reached by boat. Knysna is synonymous with oysters and in July some 300,000 or so of the delicacies are devoured during the Knysna Oyster Festival. Once a port for the timber trade, Knysna harbour today no longer functions in this capacity. With no less than 87 shipwrecks on its seabed small wonder that ships docking here were refused insurance. Today it is a marina for yachts, fishing and pleasure cruise boats.

SIGHTSEEING

FEATHERBED NATURE RESERVE ★ ☃
Magnificent nature reserve perched on top of the sandstone cliffs at the lagoon estuary with a view of the shipwrecks in the ocean. Find out about the multifaceted tours or enjoy a leisurely sunset dinner cruise on the lagoon in South Africa's only paddle steamer. Be sure to book in advance in season! *Tours daily 8.45am–6.15pm, lunch & dinner cruises leave 12.15pm and 6.15pm | 90–440 rand (depending on*

AN END TO WHALING

The Garden Route is the stretch of coast where you will see Southern Right whales. Their name goes back to the days when they were commercially hunted. These beautiful mammals are slow swimmers and float even once they have been harpooned which meant that they could easily be towed the 'right'

way, hence the name. South Africa was the first country in the world to ban whaling and by 1986 the International Whaling Commission had banned commercial whaling worldwide. Whale numbers have since increased. In November the Southern Right whales return to the cold waters of the Antarctic.

Picturesque holiday homes line the Knysna lagoon

tour/cruise) | tel. 044 3 82 16 93 | www. featherbed.co.za

THE HEADS ☼

Outside Knysna heading in the direction of Plettenberg Bay on the N 2 you will see a signpost for *The Heads*. You can drive right to the top of these landmark sandstone cliffs with your car. Breathtaking views of the lagoon from various viewing points. You may see a *dassie* or two run across your path. They may look a little like a large guinea pig but as unlikely as it may seem, their closest relative is in fact the elephant.

FOOD & DRINK

FIRE FLY EATING HOUSE

Foodies will drive all the way to this restaurant for the *bobotie* and the liquorice ice cream. Mother and daughter team Sanchia and Dell Hadlow are the spice girls of the Garden Route and will tantalise your taste buds with dishes from their travels to Asia and East Africa. Reservations essential! *152 a Old Cape Route | tel. 044 3 82 14 90 | www.fireflyeatinghouse. com | Moderate*

KNYSNA OYSTER CO.

Discover the difference between wild and cultivated oysters while sipping a glass of white wine. *Daily 9am–9pm | Thesen Island | tel. 044 3 82 69 42 | Moderate*

INSIDER TIP ▶ PHANTOM FOREST

Expect to be wowed! An off road vehicle will collect you for an evening of fine wining and dining in the depths of the Knysna forest with stunning sea view. *Phantom Forest* also offers accommodation. *Phantom Pass, west of Knysna off the N 2 | tel. 044 3 86 00 46 | Expensive*

INFORMATION

KNYSNA TOURISM

40 Main St | tel. 044 3 82 55 10 | www. visitknysna.com

Time out on Plettenberg Bay's pristine beach

PLETTENBERG BAY

(133 E6) (*ⓜ X18*) **South Africans call this enchanting village (pop. 10,000) 'Plett' and not only is it increasingly becoming** *the* **holiday destination for locals from Johannesburg but also the playground of the rich and famous.**

July and November is when the whales from the Antarctic arrive in Plettenberg Bay and with a bit of luck you may even be able to watch them giving birth to their young.

SIGHTSEEING

ROBBERG ISLAND NATURE RESERVE

Hiking paths wind through the peninsula's unspoilt coastal nature reserve and take you past caves, rocky cliffs and beaches – you may even be able to spot seals, dolphins and whales. *Entrance 25 rand | 4 km/2.4mi south of Plettenberg Bay | www.capenature.org.za*

FOOD & DRINK

LE BISTRO ON THE BAY

Light French cuisine complemented by charming décor. *Daily 8am–4pm | Lookout Centre | Main St | tel. 044 5 33 13 90 | Budget*

SPORTS & ACTIVITIES

AVENTURA ECO PLETTENBERG

If you feel adventurous you can join a guided boat trip up the Keurbooms River lasting several days which will also take you through a deep ravine. The organisers run a lodge with 29 timber cabins. *6 km/ 3.7mi east of Plettenberg Bay on the N 2 | tel. 044 5 35 93 09*

BEACHES

Plettenberg Bay's main beaches are called *Central* and *Hobie* but slightly out of town is INSIDER TIP *Keurboomstrand* (signposted if you head east on the N 2) a backdrop of rugged rock faces and a pristine beach but to take care when you go for a swim as there are some strong currents!

WHERE TO STAY

SOUTHERN CROSS BEACH HOUSE
This beautiful country style colonial house is located right on the beach. *5 rooms | 1 Capricorn Lane |tel. 044 5 33 38 68 | www. southerncross beach.co.za | Moderate*

INFORMATION

PLETTENBERG BAY TOURISM ASSOCIATION
Shop 35, Melville's Corner | Main Street | tel. 044 5 33 40 65 | www.plettenbergbay. co.za

WHERE TO GO

JEFFREY'S BAY (133 F6) (*Ø Y18*)
A two hour drive east of Plettenberg Bay is South Africa's surfing Mecca. The past few years have seen Jeffrey's Bay rapidly expanding around the surfing scene with all the stores right on trend. You may even want to give surfing a go yourself and there are a number of surfing schools to help you get started. The surf at Jeffrey's Bay is so appealing because the waves here roll in very evenly – straight, long and hollow – unlike anywhere else on this coast. Sizeable swells ensure that there is a challenge even for the most expert surfer. In July it does indeed become the domain of the expert when the world's surfing greats vie against one another in the international *Billabong Pro*. A festive time with weekend concerts in the bars! *www.jeffreysbaytourism.org*

TSITSIKAMMA NATIONAL PARK ★
(133 F6) (*Ø Y18*)
This nature reserve, located 70km/43mi from Plettenberg Bay, encompasses a coastal stretch of some 100km/62mi. By far its most beautiful section is the mouth of the Storm's River. Let the visitors' centre advise you on the best routes. There are also some fantastic accommodation options in the park but be sure to book these well in advance. Take the R 102 on your way to the park. A stop at the pristine INSIDER TIP *Nature's Valleys* beach is a must but for the ultimate adrenalin kick take the N 2 on your return journey. Here you will come face to face with the world's highest bungee jump – 216 m/708ft – from the *Bloukrans Bridge (daily 9am– 5pm)*. At the exit east of the bridge you can join a guided walking tour across the bridge. *Tsitsikamma National Park | entrance fee 108 rand per person www.san parks.org*

LOW BUDGET

▶ Cosy: *Buffalo Bay Backpackers* in Knysna (133 E6) (*Ø X18*) with a view of an endless stretch of beach. They will also arrange surfing and canoe excursions for you. *Dormitory from 80 rand, double room from 200 rand, camping 40 rand | 1 Main Rd | Buffalo Bay | tel. 044 3 83 06 08 | www.buffalobaybackpackers.co.za*

▶ Basic but charming: *Southern Comfort Western Horse Ranch* (133 E6) (*Ø X18*) even has some beds in tree houses and their guided horseback tours through the forest are also recommended. *Dormitory from 80 rand, double room from 220 rand, riding excursions from 150 rand | signposted on the N 2 between Knysna and Plettenberg Bay | tel. 044 5 32 78 85 | www.schranch.co.za*

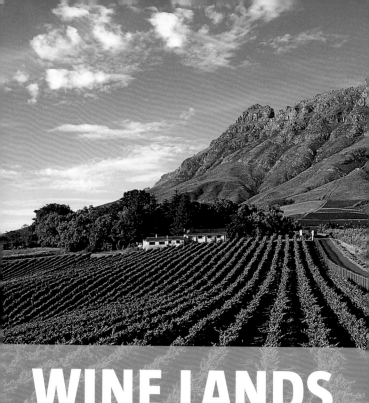

WINE LANDS

MAP INSIDE BACK COVER

On a clear day you can see the wine land mountain range all the way from Cape Town – a silhouette in the south-east beckoning you inland. Take the one hour drive from central Cape Town and head out to these majestic mountains. Up close they are even more impressive and form a magnificent backdrop to the lush green vineyards that surround them.

There are more than 150 wine estates spread across the wine lands surrounding the towns of Stellenbosch, Paarl and Franschhoek. The oldest go back as far as the 17th century when the first governor of the Cape, Jan van Riebeek, realised that the area's climatic conditions were perfect for vineyards. The area was then given even greater impetus by his successor Simon van der Stel – Stellenbosch was named after him – and newly settled French Huguenots who brought with them their grape expertise and served to give the region its wine farm fame. Today more than a billion litres of wine are produced in the area every year. The valley soil, at the foot of the mountains, is exceptionally fertile and the wine farmers have learnt to reap its potential with generations of families practising the art of viticulture over the years. Even if wine tasting is not your thing an excursion to

Photo: Mountains and vineyards that seem to go on forever

In the Cape wine lands you can experience some superb wines or simply allow yourself to be intoxicated by the enchanting landscape

the area will be well worth it. The region is protected from the wind by the surrounding mountains making it sheltered and warmer than the coast. Plan for at least two to three days to explore the wine lands as the area has some charming little villages where time seems to have stood still, villages like McGregor with its small, whitewashed thatched cottages reminiscent of colonial times.

Wine tasting is offered by most of the wine estates (as a rule a wine tasting can cost between 30 and 40 rand). Some of the wine farms also offer tasting sessions of their own cheeses or will take you around their vineyards. The wine lands are also renowned for some of the country's best restaurants and for some of the most magnificent views in the Cape, especially from the surrounding mountain passes.

The area is geared towards tourism and there are numerous wine tours that will take you from farm to farm (find out more from the brochures obtainable at Tourist Information). Wine connoisseurs can also chose a specialist tour run by industry experts, enquire at the **INSIDER TIP** *Wine Desk* at the Clock Tower Tourist Information at the V&A Waterfront *(daily 9am–*

Even though it cannot compete with Stellenbosch's architectural beauty, this small town in the heart of the wine lands is a must. It is in a lush valley perfectly nestled right below some magnificent mountains and it is also the Western Cape gourmet capital with the local trout farms supplying the restaurants with this regional delicacy.

Harvest time – South Africa's grapes produce world class wines

9pm | tel. 021 4 05 45 50 | www.winedesk waterfront.co.za). Staff here organise day trips. The tour guides are graduates from the Cape Wine Academy which also organises trips where you can join in the harvest and even stomp the grapes.

FRANSCH-HOEK

(132 B5) *(*∅ *U17)* **A little corner of France in South Africa. The Franschhoek village (population of 4000) was founded in 1688 by Huguenots who fled religious persecution in France.**

SIGHTSEEING

FRANSCHHOEK PASS ★

The narrow bends of this pass may take some negotiating but once at the top you will be rewarded with the most breathtaking views of the valley. The locals call it 'Elephant Pass' because during Huguenot times migrating elephants trampled down a path between Franschhoek and Villiersdorp.

FOOD & DRINK

LA PETITE FERME

There are the most wonderful views across the entire Franschhoek valley from the terrace of this restaurant so enjoy them with your trout or one of their delicious Cape Malay specialities. *Daily noon–4pm | Franschhoek Pass | tel. 021 8 76 30 16 | Moderate*

LE QUARTIER FRANÇAIS

Don't despair if you cannot decide which of the exquisite dishes to choose. You can always order a tasting menu. They come in different price categories and each course has a wine paired with it. Stay on after your meal and sink into one of the red armchairs in their small **INSIDER TIP** private cinema and enjoy a movie classic. *Daily from 7pm | 16 Huguenot Rd | tel. 021 8 76 21 51 | Expensive*

REUBEN'S ★

Reuben Riffel is one of the stars of the South African culinary scene and his restaurant won several awards shortly after opening. Riffel is renowned for his clever fusion of local cuisine with international specialities. *Daily 9am–3pm and 7pm–9pm | Oude Stallen Centre | 19 Huguenot Rd | tel. 021 8 76 37 72 | Moderate*

ENTERTAINMENT

LA MOTTE

On weekends classical concerts are held in this elegant wine cellar. Renowned artists are always keen to accept an invite by owner Hanneli Koegelenberg – a mezzo-soprano herself – to play here. Wine and snacks served. *Entrance fee 125 rand (includes finger food after the concert) | 6 km/3.7mi outside town (on the R 45) |tel. 021 8 76 31 19 | www.la-motte.com*

WHERE TO STAY

LA FONTAINE GUEST HOUSE

This historic villa has been lovingly restored and there is also a pool. The rooms

are all tastefully and individually decorated with the most beautiful antiques. Delicious buffet breakfast. *12 rooms, 1 family suite | 12 Dirkie Uys St | tel. 021 8 76 21 12 | www.lafontainefranschhoek.co.za | Budget*

INFORMATION

FRANSCHHOEK VALLÉE TOURISM BUREAU
70 Huguenot St | tel. 021 8 76 36 03 | www.franschhoek.org.za

WHERE TO GO

BOSCHENDAL (132 B5) (U17)
One of South Africa's oldest and most beautiful wine farms some 20 km/12.4mi from Franschhoek. The Cape Dutch wine cellar dates back to 1685 and the original manor house is a national monument. The manor house cellar has been converted into a fine dining restaurant. At **INSIDER TIP** *Le Café* you should try the

MARCO POLO HIGHLIGHTS

estate's famous Blanc de Noir. *Daily 8.30am–5pm | Pniel Road | Groot Drakenstein | tel. 021 8 70 42 00*

PAARL

(132 B5) (𝄞 U17) On the banks of the Berg River, it is named after the Peerlbergh, a massive 700 m/2296ft high granite rock that shimmers like a pearl when the sun catches it.

The heart of Paarl (population of 88,000) is Main Street with its Victorian houses and churches. Paarl is also home to the world's largest wine and brandy cooperative KWV (Kooperatieve Wijnbouwers Vereniging) and is a very historic town. It is here where the world's youngest language, Afrikaans was declared an official language in 1875, the same year when the first Afrikaans daily 'Die Afrikaanse Patriot' was printed. Nelson Mandela also spent the last years of his imprisonment here.

SIGHTSEEING

PAARL MOUNTAIN NATURE RESERVE

This national park surrounds the town's iconic landmark – the 500 million year old granite mass of Paarl Rock. The views from the rock are quite something and anyone can walk up it but only seasoned climbers should attempt the steep sections. *Oct–March daily 7am–7pm, April–Sept 7am–6pm | entrance fee Sat/Sun 23 rand per car and 6 rand per person, entrance free of charge Mon–Fri, | tel. 021 8 72 36 58*

WINE ESTATES

FAIRVIEW

Famed for its exceptional sheep, cow and goat's milk cheeses, so you should reserve a table at the café and choose your own selection of a INSIDER TIP delectable cheese platter at a reasonable price! *Mon–Fri 8.30am–5pm, Sat 8.30am–4pm, Sun 9.30am–4pm | Suid Agter Paarl Rd | Suiderpaarl | tel. 021 8 63 24 50*

KWV ★

Tours of the *Kooperatieve Wijnbouwers Vereniging* founded in 1918 begin with a documentary on the wine production process. You are then led through the huge wine cellars of the estate (privately managed since 1997) followed by a tasting session of the excellent wines and brandies for which this cooperative is renowned. *Tours Mon–Sat 10am and 10.30am, Sun 11 am | 30 rand | Kohler Street | tel. 021 8 07 30 07*

LOW BUDGET

▶ Excellent value for money: ☙ *Banghoek Place* is an upmarket backpacker hostel in Stellenbosch **(132 B5–6) (𝄞 U17–18)** with an excellent view of Simonsberg. There is a pool in the garden and it is also not far from the beach, approx. 20 minutes. *3 dormitories, 13 rooms | 193 Banghoek Rd | tel. 021 8 87 00 48 | www.banghoek.co.za*

▶ Every Friday a jazz combo plays ☙ in the garden of the *Vineyard Brasserie* in Franschhoek **(132 B5) (𝄞 U17)**. Enjoy the music, freshly baked bread and local cheeses while you sip your glass of wine, wonderful views of the Boland Mountains. The entrance fee of 120 rand includes a bottle of wine. *Fri 5.30pm–8.30pm | 13 Daniel Hugo St | tel. 021 8 76 21 55*

Maturing into some of the finest wines at the KWV cellar in Paarl

PONTAC MANOR
The hotel lies on a former wine estate and you will be staying in one of Paarl's oldest farm houses. *23 rooms | 16 Zion Street | tel. 021 8 72 04 45 | www.pontac.com | Moderate*

PAARL TOURISM BUREAU
216 Main St | tel. 021 8 72 08 60 | www. paarlonline.com

DIEMERSFONTEIN (132 B5) *(ɯ U17)*
This wine farm in neighbouring Wellington, some 15 km/9.3 mi from Paarl, offers horseback riding tours from farm to farm and if you are up to it, from wine tasting to wine tasting. *On the R 301 between Wellington and Paarl | 180 rand/hr | reservations 021 8 64 50 50*

STELLEN-BOSCH

MAP INSIDE BACK COVER
(132 B5–6) *(ɯ U17–18)* **The heart of the wine lands: its picturesque and historic village centre is surrounded by wide avenues lined with magnificent 300 year old oak trees.**

That is how Stellenbosch (pop. 80,000) got its Afrikaans nickname: Eikestad. More than 100 of its 18th and 19th century Cape Dutch buildings are listed national monuments. The town is named after Cape governor Simon van der Stel who founded it as a settlement on the Eerste River in 1679.

DIE BRAAK
This square in the town centre once served as parade grounds and it is surrounded

by many historical buildings that previously belonged to the VOC. Explore the interesting streets that lead off it: Church, Dorp und Ryneveld with their galleries, cafés and small boutiques. Here you will also find the *Old Lutheran Church* dating back to 1851, distinctive for its neo-Gothic style. Today it houses the university's art gallery.

Journey back in time – the Village Museum in Stellenbosch

INSIDER TIP JONKERSHOEK NATURE RESERVE

This isolated valley on the edge of town hides cascading waterfalls and peaceful lakes, explore them by taking one of the hiking trails. *Open all year daily 8am–6pm | entrance fee 20 rand | Jonkershoek Valley*

VILLAGE MUSEUM

Four houses perfectly restored to their original state give you an insight into the various eras in Stellenbosch's history. One of them, *Schreuderhuis*, was built in 1709 and is South Africa's oldest town house.

Mon–Sat 9am–5pm, Sun 10am–4pm | 18 Ryneveld St | tel. 021 8 87 29 48

WINE ESTATES

ERNIE ELS WINES ●

Former South African golfing pro Ernie Els has established one of the most idyllic wine estates in the region. Completed in 2004, this fully established estate has unrivalled views across the Helderberg Mountain and has won him the services of coveted winemaker Louis Strydom. Its architecture may be modern and contemporary but the atmosphere is warm and inviting. Tasting sessions include seven wines and cost 40 rand per person. *Annandale Road | tel. 02 18 81 35 88 | www.ernieelswines.com*

SPIER

This estate is one of the few that is geared towards families. The children can ride ponies while the parents relax with a lovely picnic. The amphitheatre regularly stages concerts and theatre performances and at *Moyo* you can indulge in the generous African buffet *(reservations tel. 021 8 09 11 33 | Expensive)* and for holidaymakers without their own transport: there is a direct train connection from Cape Town. *Daily 9am–5pm | around 310 rand | tel. 021 8 09 11 00 | www.spier.co.za*

UITKYK

There is no better estate for a picnic than Uitkyk. True to its Afrikaans name you get the most beautiful view of the forests and meadows when you picnic on the lawns in front of the manor house. You may catch the faint strains of some piano music – the picnic basket packers swear that a ghost has been tickling the ivories here for years. *Mon–Fri 9am–5pm, Sat/Sun 10am–4pm (reservations the day before) | on the R 44 | tel. 021 8 84 44 16 | www.uitkyk.co.za*

FOOD & DRINK

96 WINERY ROAD

This restaurant is just outside of town on the Zandberg Farm. Sit out on the terrace and enjoy the lovely surroundings while you indulge in their excellent Karoo lamb. The sommelier will help you pair your meal with the right wine. *Daily noon–3pm, Mon–Sat from 7pm | Zandberg Farm | Winery Rd | on the R 44 | tel. 021 8 42 20 20 | Moderate*

TOKARA ☙

A restaurant with very dramatic views in a building that is as chic and as contemporary as its menu. A delight for those who enjoy exotic delicacies – expect to be wowed with some unexpected combinations like mussels served with apples and hibiscus. *Tue–Sat noon–3pm and from 7pm | Helshoogte Pass | tel. 021 8 08 59 59 | Expensive*

WHERE TO STAY

LANZERAC MANOR

Located on a 300 year old wine estate in the magical Jonkershoek Valley, with luxury accommodation in the Cape Dutch style. *48 rooms | Lanzerac Rd | tel. 021 8 87 11 32 | www.lanzerac.co.za | Expensive*

INFORMATION

STELLENBOSCH TOURISM BUREAU

36 Market St | tel. 021 8 83 35 84 | www.stellenboschtourism.co.za

WHERE TO GO

VERGELEGEN ★
(132 B6) (*♕ U18*)

A tour to the wine lands is always part of any visiting dignitary's Cape Town itinerary and Vergelegen is invariably the destination of choice. The estate is on the outskirts of Somerset West, some 15 km/9.3mi from Stellenbosch. It is stunningly beautiful – with its idyllic English rose garden, majestic old trees and expansive lawns – and it also holds a wealth of historical information. There is, for example, a library with some 4500 volumes on its shelves some going back to the 17th century. A special treat in the afternoon is INSIDER TIP *Lady Phillips Tea Garden* where you can sit amongst the rose bushes and enjoy a wonderful cup of tea with a freshly baked slice of cake *(reservations tel. 021 8 47 13 46). Daily 9.30am–4pm | Lourensford Rd | Somerset West | tel. 021 8 47 13 34 | www.vergelegen.co.za*

PAARL WALK TO FREEDOM

Nelson Mandela did not spend the final years of his imprisonment on Robben Island, but in a house on the Groot Drakenstein Prison premises in Paarl. However, the prison on the R 301 between Paarl and Franschhoek had a different name at the time: Victor Verster Prison. The ruling National Party government transferred him to the more comfortable facility as a sign of good will. Mandela took to the architecture of the building so much that, after he was released on 11 February 1990, he had a replica built in his home town of Qunu near Umtata in the former Transkei. Since the prison surrounding the building where he was housed is still a correctional facility, is not possible to visit the final station of Nelson Mandela's walk to freedom.

FESTIVALS & EVENTS

Capetonians are as keen on their sport as they are on their fun and they celebrate with carnivals, cycle and road races and markets – there is always something on no matter when you decide to visit.

PUBLIC HOLIDAYS

The following are public (bank) holidays when government offices, post offices, businesses but not necessarily all shops are closed: **1 Jan** *New Year's Day*; **21 March** *Human Rights Day*; **March/April** *Good Friday, Easter Sunday, Family Day (Easter Monday)* **27 April** *Freedom Day*; **1 May** *Workers' Day*; **16 June** *Youth Day*; **9 Aug** *National Women's Day*; **24 Sept** *Heritage Day*; **16 Dec** *Day of Reconciliation*; **25 Dec** *Christmas Day* **26 Dec** *Day of Goodwill*. In the event of a public holiday falling on a Sun the following Mon is a public holiday.

FESTIVALS & EVENTS

JANUARY

▶ ★ *Cape Town Minstrel Carnival:* takes place in the first few days of January and it has a long tradition. The slaves had to work on New Year but were given the following day off to celebrate. Today it is the custom of the coloured community to dress in bright minstrel gear with parasols, the troops then dance and sing their way through the streets.

▶ INSIDER TIP *J&B Met:* the society event of the year. The country's most prestigious horse race is held at the Kenilworth Race Course on the last Sunday – a day when thousands don extravagant hats and outfits and showcase Cape Town's most outlandish designers. *www.jbmet.co.za*

MARCH

▶ *Cape Argus Cycle Tour:* the 109km/67.7mi race around the peninsula is popular with young and old, professionals and families alike and is the largest timed cycle event in the world. *www.cycletour.co.za*

MARCH/APRIL

▶ *Two Oceans Marathon:* one of the world's most stunning routes, this 56 km/34.7mi ultra marathon across the peninsula has scenic sections along the coast. Always falls on the Easter weekend. *www.twooceansmarathon.org.za*

What better way to send off the New Year than with a carnival: find out what's on in and around Cape Town at a glance

▶ *Cape Town International Jazz Festival:* national and international music greats transform Cape Town into a jazz Mecca on the first weekend of the month. Additional events include free concerts and jazz workshops. *www.capetownjazzfest.com*

MAY–OCTOBER
▶ *Whale migration:* in the winter months whales from the Antarctic arrive on the coast to give birth to their young. Some come so close to shore that you can watch them from a few feet away. There are numerous whale watching tour organisations.

JULY
▶ ★ *Oyster Festival* in Knysna: up to 200,000 oysters are consumed at this festival with highlights like oyster-shucking and oyster eating competitions. Plenty of support events if you are not an oyster fan. *www.oysterfestival.co.za*

SEPTEMBER/OCTOBER
▶ *Cape Town International Comedy Festival:* for a good laugh visit several venues in the city playing host to the international comedians. *www.comedyfestival.co.za*
▶ *Cape Town Oktoberbierfest:* a German beer festival that will transport you to the heart of Bavaria. Wooden benches, waitresses in dirndls, an oompah band in lederhosen all recreate the beer halls in Munich. They also serve German home-brewed beer and plenty of it. Check the exact dates and venue at *www.oktoberbierfest.co.za.*

DECEMBER
▶ *Mother City Queer Project:* a huge gay party with a different theme every year, participants all sport outlandish outfits.
▶ *Adderley Street Night Market:* in the days prior to Christmas the cars on Adderley Street give way to a festively lit night market with stalls and music.

LINKS, BLOGS, APPS & MORE

LINKS

▶ www.capetown.travel In terms of quality, this is one of the best websites on tourism in Cape Town

▶ www.021magazine.co.za A whole lot of tips about what is on – with a calendar for arts, music, sports and cultural events

▶ dailymaverick.co.za Daily posts by authors with a good insight into South African society

▶ www.tripadvisor.com As is in many countries, the world's largest travel site, is active here and provides tourists with reliable reviews and advice from real travellers. The destination experts in particular are well qualified

BLOGS & FORUMS

▶ www.empirecafe.co.za/blog Entertaining blog by the owner (and surf fanatic) of the *Empire Café*, with entries on anything from food to lifestyle, to topics of general interest – of course surfing is a hot topic

▶ capetownblog.co.za Interesting lifestyle blog by Cape Town residents who submit articles about the Mother City

▶ www.grootbos.com/en/blog *Grootbos Private Nature Reserve* is a five-star establishment a few hours outside Cape Town. The blog has an emphasis on nature conservation and responsible tourism, a priority that comes through in its postings on life in one of the most beautiful areas in the Cape

VIDEOS & STREAMS

▶ www.youtube.com/user/CapeTownTourism Makes available videos of Cape Town's attractions and events online

▶ www.youtube.com/user/capetownbackpack?ob= A video blog with interview clips of volunteers from GCU, a community organisation that helps

Regardless of whether you are still preparing your trip or already in Cape Town: these addresses will provide you with more information, videos and networks to make your holiday even more enjoyable

to tutor and mentor children in one of the city's most impoverished areas.

VIDEOS & STREAMS

▶ www.youtube.com/user/mang wanani?feature=chclk Audio clips of some of the prank calls made by one of South Africa's most popular radio DJs, Whackhead Simpson on his show on Highveld 94.7

APPS

▶ Cape Town Walking Tours and Map This app has some of the best city walks to help you to explore the city and locate sites and once you have downloaded it works offline

▶ Computicket For concert, sports and theatre production tickets and dates

▶ Star Walk In Cape Town the night sky can be very clear; this app determines your exact position. You simply point your device and it gives you the starscape above you

▶ Afrikaans Speak Board In Cape Town everyone speaks English but this easy to use app has some essential phrases to help you to speak perfect Afrikaans

▶ FlightTrack Pro Follow your flight status in real time. Very helpful during long hauls and for connecting flights

NETWORK

▶ www.facebook.com/bayharbour Impressions of Bay Harbour Market one of the city's nicest markets

▶ http://twitter.com/#!/capetowntourism The official twitter account for Cape Town Tourism with tweets about cultural events, specials, weekly highlights and some beautiful photographs

▶ www.airbnb.com Airbnb is the popular site for travellers who prefer to stay in private accommodation offered by locals. A search under Cape Town pulls up the full spectrum from a deluxe penthouse with uninterrupted views of the Atlantic through to a renovated Victorian cottage in the historic Cape Quarter area. The site is constantly updated with new listings and user reviews

TRAVEL TIPS

ARRIVAL

🛬 *South African Airways (www.flysaa. com)* has regular scheduled flights to Cape Town from most major international cities. Some airlines regularly offer specials so it is worth taking a look other airlines like *British Airways (www.british-airways. com)* and *Emirates (www.emirates.com)*. The cheapest fares are in the South African winter between April and September the most popular (and expensive) are in summer from December to May. Cape Town International Airport is 23km/14.2mi from the city centre. All the main car hire companies are represented at the airport. It is always a good idea to book your vehicle in advance so it is ready on arrival. There is also the public *Myciti* bus to central Cape Town or you can use a private shuttle bus service *(e.g City Hopper | tel. 021 3 86 00 77 | from 160 rand per person)*. Flight information: *tel. 086 7 27 78 88 | www.airports.co.za*

RESPONSIBLE TRAVEL

It doesn't take a lot to be environmentally friendly whilst travelling. Don't just think about your carbon footprint whilst flying to and from your holiday destination but also about how you can protect nature and culture abroad. As a tourist it is especially important to respect nature, look out for local products, cycle instead of driving, save water and much more. If you would like to find out more about eco-tourism please visit: *www.ecotourism.org*

CAR HIRE

Since Cape Town still lacks a comprehensive public transport commuter system it is advisable to hire a car to get around. The minimum age to hire a car is 23 and an international driver's licence is a prerequisite. In most instances you will have had to be in possession of a driver's license for at least two years. The contact details of the main outlets are: *Avis (tel. 0861 11 37 48 | www.avis.co.za)*, *Budget (tel. 011 3 98 01 23 | www.budget.co.za)*, *Europcar (tel. 0861 13 10 00 | www.europcar.co.za)* and *Hertz (tel. 0861 60 01 36 | www.hertz. co.za)*. Cheaper rates are offered by INSIDER TIP *Panorama Tours*: the agency buys entire quotas from the big car rental companies and resells them at a cheaper rate *(tel. 021 4 26 16 34 | www.panorama tours.co.za)*. Cape Town also has its own local car hire companies like *Around about Cars (20 Bloem St | tel. 021 4 22 40 22 | www.aroundaboutcars.com | from 250 rand/day)* and you can even hire a scooter or vintage car: at INSIDER TIP *Café Vespa* you can enjoy a latte macchiato then ride off on a Vespa *(108 Kloof St | Gardens | tel. 021 4 26 50 42 | www.cafevespa.com | from 200 rand/day)*. Take your pick at *Motor Classic*. Will it be a 1968 model Jaguar or a 1984 Porsche Carrera? *1 Waterloo St, behind the Ferrari building, Roeland St | Vredehoek | tel. 021 4 61 73 68 | www.motor classic.co.za | from 690 rand/day*.

CLIMATE, WHEN TO GO

The seasons in Cape Town are the reverse of those in the northern hemisphere. The warmest months average 25°C/77°F during the day and are from December to

From arrival to weather

Holiday from start to finish: the most important addresses and information for your Cape Town trip

March, the most popular tourism months are from September to April. The Cape has a very pleasant Mediterranean climate with dry summers and winter rainfalls.

CONSULATES & EMBASSIES

BRITISH CONSULATE GENERAL
Southern Life Centre | 15th Floor | 8 Riebeeck St Cape Town | tel. +27 2 14 05 24 00 |

US CONSULATE
2 Reddam Ave | Westlake | Cape Town | tel. +27 21 702 73 00

CUSTOMS

Among others the following goods can be imported duty-free to South Africa: 1L spirits, 400 cigarettes and goods not exceeding 200 rand in value. The following goods can be imported duty-free into the EU: 1L spirits, 200 cigarettes, 2L wine and goods not exceeding a total of 390 pounds in value. Do not take a risk by exporting protected plant and animal species or their products. It is strictly prohibited by law. By the same token the importation of seeds and plants is also not permitted. For more information go to *www.visahq.com/customs*

DRIVING

PARKING
In the city centre parking monitors wearing blue uniforms patrol designated areas on the streets. If you park here you pay the monitor in advance (7 rand/hr). Should you get back to your car after an hour you won't be towed away nor will you get a fine. Simply pay the balance when you get

BUDGETING

Cable car	£14.5/$23 *return ticket*
Filter coffee	£1.30/$2 *per cup*
Wine	£1.60/$2.50 *by the glass*
Biltong	£2.60/$4.20 *150 g packet of tear strips*
Boerewors	£1/$1.50 *for a boerewors roll*
Wood giraffe	£25–60/$40–100 *depending on size*

there. If you park on the streets at night and outside the city centre there are usually informal car guards who will let you know they will look after your car. Most of them don't wear uniforms, only a yellow vest. They work contractually and will not ask for payment. Because the streets actually have become safer thanks to them, drivers will generally honour their work with a 4 to 5 rand tip.

SPEED LIMITS
120/h km on the motorway, 80 km/h on rural roads, 60 km/h in the city.

TRAFFIC
In South Africa you drive on the left hand side. Be vigilant as not everyone keeps to the traffic rule that you can only overtake on the right. As bizarre as this may sound to visitors: watch out for cyclists and pedestrians on the motorway. Petrol stations should accept credit cards but best to check before you fill up.

ELECTRICITY

220 Volt/50 cycles per second. Three pronged plugs with round pins are the norm so you may require an adapter. Hotels will generally be able to provide one and supermarkets sell them.

EMERGENCY SERVICES

From a land line: Police *10 111;* ambulance *10 177;* from a mobile phone: *112*

HEALTH

You don't need vaccinations for Cape Town and surrounds and you will only need malaria prophylaxis if you are going up north. Cape Town's privately run hospitals are state-of-the-art and their health care world class. It is important that you take out appropriate travel insurance. NHS or government health insurance certificates from other countries are not accepted and you have to pay your bill right away. In case of emergency, central Cape Town's closest facility is: *Mediclinic (21 Hof St | Oranjezicht | tel. 021 4 64 55 55).* Incidentally it is safe to drink Cape Town's tap water.

IMMIGRATION

Visitors entering South Africa must be in possession of a valid passport and visitors from the EU, USA, Australia and New Zealand do not require a visa for a stay of 90 days or less. Passports must be valid for six months and should have at least two unused pages.

INFORMATION

SOUTH AFRICAN TOURISM UK
6 Alt Grove London SW19 4DZ. Call centre 0870 1550 044 | www.southafrica.net/ sat/content/en/uk/uk-home

SOUTH AFRICAN TOURISM US
500 5th Avenue 20th Floor, Suite 2040, New York NY 10110. Call centre 1 800 593 1318 |www.southafrica.net/sat/content/ en/us/us- home

GENERAL INFORMATION
Tourist Information in Cape Town provides an excellent service when it comes to booking sports & activities, trips & tours and where to go in the evening:
– *City Centre | Mon–Fri 8am–6pm, Sat 8.30am–2pm, Sun 9am–1pm | corner Burg St/Castle St | Central* (129 D4) (*ⓜ G4*) *| tel. +27 21 4 87 68 00*
– *V & A Waterfront | Clock Tower* (129 E1) (*ⓜ G2*) *| daily 9am–9pm | tel. +27 21 4 05 45 00*
Official tourism website: *www.tourism capetown.co.za*

ADDITIONAL INFORMATION
Accommodation: *www.portfoliocollection. com;* restaurant recommendations: *www. eatout.co.za;* overview of what's hot in the pop and classical music scene: *www. overtone.co.za;* events bookings: *www. computicket.com*

INTERNET CAFÉS & WI-FI

The rates at internet cafés in the city centre, Long Street or on the V&A Waterfront can be steep *(15 rand/30 minutes). African Access* in Observatory is much cheaper *(daily 9am–midnight | 50 Lower Main Rd | tel. 021 4 48 71 10).* Many cafés now offer Wi-Fi access but rarely for free.

MEDIA

Cape Town has two local dailies: the 'Cape Times' and the 'Cape Argus', with the national 'Mail & Guardian' appearing weekly on a Friday. The latter is an excellent source of information on restaurants, bars and what's on. 'Cape Unplugged' is a free monthly newspaper with good tips on alternative events in the city and surrounds. Bars, backpackers and car rentals are where you are likely to find a copy. 'The next 48 hours' is also free of charge and has the best pointers on cultural highlights and what's on in Cape Town over the next few days. Collect your copy at *Cape Town Tourism Visitor Information Centre*.

MONEY & CREDIT CARDS

You can withdraw cash using your Visa, MasterCard or debit card at most ATMs but avoid drawing money in isolated areas and don't let strangers 'help' you. The safest places are shopping malls and petrol stations where there are security staff on duty. Pay for your purchases by credit card, most restaurants and hotels accept credit cards. If you lose your card banks will be able to assist you with ordering a replacement. All banks will cash travellers' cheques. Bank opening times: Mon–Fri 9am–3.30pm, Sat 9am to 11am. Emergency no. if your credit card goes missing: *American Express 0800 11 09 29; Master Card 800 99 04 18; Visa 0800 99 04 75*

OPENING TIMES

The shops in central Cape Town close at 5pm on a weekday, 1pm on a Saturday. Shops in malls such as the V&A Waterfront and Canal Walk stay open as late as 9pm. Most supermarkets close between 8pm and 9pm. There is always the *Friendly 7 Eleven* which remains open from 7am to 11pm every day for those last minute grocery items. On a Sunday generally only shops in shopping malls and supermarkets are open but they are not allowed sell any alcohol and seal off those aisles.

PHONE & MOBILE PHONE

You will always dial ten digits to make a call locally (land line numbers all include the city code). You can hire a mobile phone at the airport on arrival or bring your own if you have confirmed with your service provider that it is compatible. Using your credit card you can rent a SIM card on arrival for around 20 rand a day and 5 rand per minute. Alternatively buy a starter pack from any cell phone service provider store: *Cell C (www.cellc.co.za), MTN (www.mtn. co.za), Vodacom (www.vodacom.co.za)*. Prepaid air time is sold at supermarkets, malls or petrol stations. You will need to show your passport and airline ticket.

The code for phoning overseas from South Africa is *00* followed by the country code, e.g. UK *00 44*, USA and Canada *001*, Australia *00 61*. The code for calling South Africa is *00 27*.

POST

Opening times: Mon–Fri 8.30am–4.30pm and Sat 8am–noon. The post office at the V&A Waterfront is also open on a Sunday until lunchtime. Postage to Europe: postcards 4.60 rand, standard letters 5.40 rand. It can be expensive to send a parcel. If you are shipping wine or bulky arts and crafts the wine estates and merchants selling them will gladly be of assistance.

PRICES & CURRENCY

The South African currency is the rand (ZAR); 1 rand = 100 cents. Coin denominations in circulation: 1, 2, 5,10, 20 and 50 cents and 1, 2 and 5 rand; note denominations: 10, 20, 50, 100 and 200 rand. The currency is stable and the exchange rate for the rand is favourable which means price levels are slightly below those in the UK and the USA.

CURRENCY CONVERTER

£	ZAR	ZAR	£
1	12.5	10	0.80
3	23	30	2.4
5	63	50	4
13	163	130	10.4
40	500	400	32
75	940	750	60
120	1500	1200	96
250	3140	2500	200
500	6280	5000	400

$	ZAR	ZAR	$
1	8	10	1.25
3	23.5	30	2.50
5	39	50	6.3
13	102	130	16.3
40	315	400	50
75	590	750	94
120	940	1200	150
250	1965	2500	313
500	3930	5000	625

For current exchange rates see www.xe.com

PUBLIC TRANSPORT

Cheap but not for the fainthearted: the commuter minibus taxis that race through the streets of Cape Town. They do specific routes, service all areas and will stop anywhere on request *(see 'In a nutshell')*. A new option is Cape Town's ever expanding *Myciti* rapid bus service which already operates on some routes. Your best bet, although a bit more pricy, is the distinctive open top red *Citysightseeing Cape Town Hop On – Hop Off* bus which operates two routes at 15 minute intervals. You pay 140 rand and can get off and back on wherever you want to. The red tour focuses on the city centre, the blue tour on the coast and the Constantia wine route and you get a sightseeing commentary (stops and bookings at *www.citysightseeing.co.za, tel. 021 5 11 60 00;* tickets also sold on the bus).

TAX & TAX REFUNDS

You are eligible to be refunded 14 per cent VAT on a purchase of 250 rand provided you can present a tax invoice. There is a refund counter at the airport and you will be reimbursed in rand. To speed up the process you may want to collect the necessary forms ahead of time at the *Visitor Information Centre* in the Clock Tower at the V & A Waterfront *(Mon–Sat 9am–5.30pm, Sun 10am–5.30pm)* or at the *Cape Town Tourism Visitor Information Centre* and complete them before you head for the airport.

TAXIS

In Cape Town the term *taxi* refers to the packed minibuses that transport commuters between the townships and the city *(see 'In a nutshell')*. For a regular taxi you need to ask for a *metered taxi*. You will find them at special taxi stands or you can phone for one *e.g. Excite (tel. 021 4 48 44 44)* or Unicab *(tel. 021 4 48 17 20)*. Besides these there are the so-called *Rikkis* that mainly collect and drop off tourists on short trips in the city centre *(tel. 086 1 74 55 47)*. Central points in the city are equipped with Rikki phones so you can call a cab free of charge.

TIME

South Africa is on Central African Time (CAT) which is one hour ahead of the UK during the South African summer and two hours during winter, it is seven hours ahead of Eastern Standard Winter Time

TIPPING

In Cape Town your bill does not include the waiter's gratuity – at least in most cases. However, some restaurants now add a 10 per cent service charge on to the bill so it is a good idea to read the small print. It is common practice to leave a tip of between 10 and 15 per cent of the total.

WELLNESS

Most of Cape Town's luxury hotels offer wellness programmes even for non guests e.g. *Suntra Spa* at the *15 on Orange Hotel* (www.suntra.co.za) or *Librisa Spa* at the *Mount Nelson Hotel* (www.mountnelson. co.za).

LONG STREET BATHS ●
(129 D5) (*ø F–G5*)

Although these baths were built in 1908 the technology is up to date and they still retain their old-world charm. *Daily 7am– 7pm | tel. 021 4 00 33 02 | Long St | Central*

CAPE TOWN MEDI-SPA ●
(128 C6) (*ø F5–6*)

Hydrotherapy with the use of floatation tanks are just one of their treatments – salt from the Dead Sea is added to the water, allowing you to stay afloat effortlessly till your body feels completely revived. They also offer ayurvedic treatments and various massages. *Mon–Fri 8.30am–5.30pm, Sat 9am–5.30pm | 250 rand/hr | tel. 021 4 22 51 40 | 99 Kloof St | Central*

WEATHER IN CAPE TOWN

	Jan	Feb	March	April	May	June	July	Aug	Sept	Oct	Nov	Dec
Daytime temperatures in °C/°F	27/81	27/81	26/79	23/73	20/68	18/64	18/64	18/64	19/66	21/70	24/75	25/77
Nighttime temperatures in °C/°F	17/63	17/63	16/61	13/55	11/52	9/48	9/48	9/48	11/52	12/54	14/57	16/61
Sunshine hours/day	11	11	10	8	7	6	6	7	8	9	10	11
Precipitation days/month	3	2	3	6	9	9	10	9	7	5	4	3
Water temperatures in °C/°F	18/64	19/66	19/66	18/64	17/63	16/61	15/59	14/57	15/59	16/61	17/63	18/64

NOTES

MARCO POLO TRAVEL GUIDES

- PACKED WITH INSIDER TIPS
- BEST WALKS AND TOURS
- FULL-COLOUR PULL-OUT MAP
  AND STREET ATLAS

STREET ATLAS

The green line ▬▬ indicates the Walking tours (p. 88–93)

All tours are also marked on the pull-out map

Photo: Chapman's Peak Drive

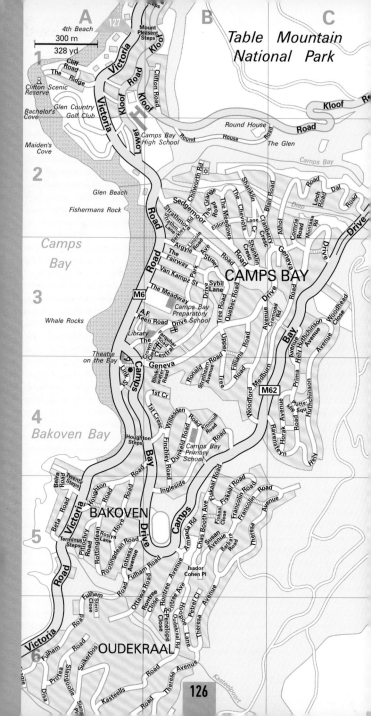

A

4th Beach

300 m
328 yd

Clifton Scenic
Reserve

Bachelor's
Cove

Maiden's
Cove

Glen Country
Golf Club

The
Ridge

Cliff
Road

Glen Beach

Fishermans Rock

Camps

Bay

Whale Rocks

Theatre
on the Bay

Bakoven Bay

BAKOVEN

B

Mount
Pleasant Steps

Victoria

Kloof

Road

Kloof

Clifton Road

Lower Kloof Road

Camps Bay
High School

Round House

Round
House

Road

The Glen

Chilworth Rd

The Grange

Sedgemoor

Strathmore

Argyle

The
Fairway

Van Kampz St

The Meadway

A.F.
Keen Road

Library

The
Central

Geneva

Blinkwater
Road

Sybil
Lane

Quebec Road

Upper

Ronald Road

Strathearn Road
Avenue

Tree

Link St.

1st Cr

1st Cres

Camps

Houghton
Steps

Beira Road

Twenty
Steps

Bay

Willesden

Road

Finchley Road

Camps Bay
Primary
School

Ingleside

Dunkeld Road

Kimmill
Road

Woodford

Road

Road

Bay

Drive

Road

Fillians Road

Medbun

M62

Woodford

Ronald

The Cheviots

The Meadows

Eldono

Shanklin
Cresc

Geneva

Road

CAMPS BAY

Bay

Avenue

Crawford
Rd

Avenue

Hutchinson

Prima

Matte Sq

Hutchinson

Hely

Ravensteyn

Horak

Avenue

Hely

Road

Woodhead
Close

Avenue

Avenue

C

*Table Mountain
National Park*

Kloof

Road

Camps Bay

Drop

Road

Road

Dal

Loch
Road

Connie
Road

Athol

Montana
Rd

Geneva

Drive

Drive

Victoria

Road

Road

BAKOVEN

Houghton
Road

Hove

Road

Terminus Steps

Pitt's
Rd

Roslyn
Lane

Rootingdean Road

Totnes

Fulham

Avenue

Camps

Drive

Finchley Road

Chas Booth Ave

Amanda Rd

Isador
Cohen Pl

Fiskaal
Close

Fiskaal Road

Fiskaal Road

Francolin Road

Francolin
Road

Susan

Avenue

Barbit
Road

Theresa

Avenue

Victoria

Road

Stern
Close

Fulham
Close

Ottawa Road

Rontree Road

Rontree
Close

Penelope
Close

Quldekraal
Lane

Rontree Ave

Petrel Ct

Theresa

Avenue

OUDEKRAAL

Fulham

Road

Proya

Suikerbos

Slangolie

Disa

Kasteells

Theresa

Avenue

Kasteelpoort

126

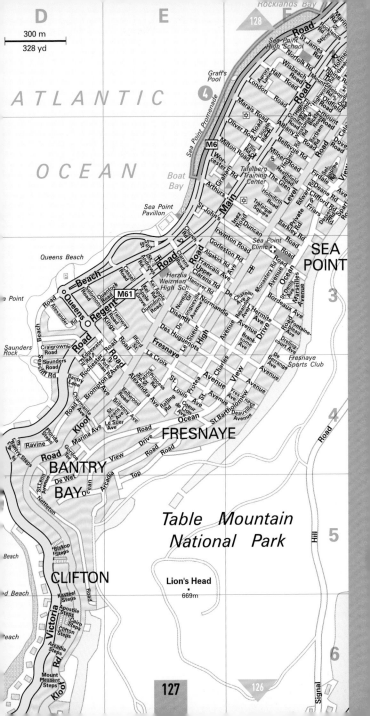

D

300 m
328 yd

A T L A N T I C

O C E A N

Queens Beach

a Point

Saunders
Rock

E

Rocklands Bay

Sea Point
High School

Graff's Pool

Sea Point Promenade

M6

Boat
Bay

Sea Point
Pavilion

Beach
Road

Queens

Regent

M61

Road

Craigrownie
Road

Saunders
Road

Seacliff Rd

Alexander

Beach
Road

St Leon
Avenue

Florida
Road

Ravine

Road

Nettleton

Bishop
Steps

CLIFTON

Beach

Kasteel
Steps

Apostle
Steps

Cairn
Steps

Clifton
Steps

Victoria

Arcadia
Steps

Mount
Pleasant
Steps

Kloof

BANTRY

BAY

De Wet

Ocean

View

Arcadia

Road

Road

Gordon

Marina Ave

Kloof

Charmante

Bantry
Lane

Road

Road

Rd

Fir

Edgewater
Rd

Rochester
Rd

Ilford
Road

Kings

Alexandra Ave

Bellwood
Road

St
Leger
Ave

Le Suer
Ave

Britanny Ave

Coeur
de Lion
Ave

Princess
Rd

St Louis
Ave

Railing
Rd

Road

Top

Brommton Ave

La Croix

Road

Fresnaye

Des Huguenots

Road

Le Sueur

Disandt

De
Lorentz

Normanville

St Bartholomew's
Avenue

Deauville
Avenue

Protea
Avenue

Charles

Avenue

View

Avenue

Ocean

Drive

FRESNAYE

Road

F

Marine Rd
Rocklands Rd

St James
Road

Road

Road

Norfolk Rd

Wisbeach
Road

Ave

London
Road

Oliver Road

Marais Road

Milton Road

Worcester
Road

Graham Rd

Arthurs

St John's

St John's

Church

Solomon's Road

Dumrrock
Road

Beach

Road

Kei Apple
Rd

Avenue

Tramway
Road

Quendon

Glengariff Rd

De

Clyde Rd

Disandt
Avenue

Normandie
Avenue

De
Chateau

Tafelberg
Training
Center

Main

Tafelberg
Training
Center

Trafalgar
Square

Francais Ave

Gorleston Rd

Irwinton Rd

Herzlia
Weizman
High Sch.

Upper
Clarens Rd

Hanover Rd

Highworth Rd
Regent Rd

De Lorentz

Aurora Rd
Hall Rd

Conifer Rd

Ellis Rd

Milner Road

Bellevue Rd

Duncan

Inez
Road

Road

Duncan

Barkley Rd

Sea Point
Clinic

Monastery Rd

Avenue

Chateau

Avenue

Avenue

Hermite
Avenue

De Villiers
Avenue

Warseilles
Avenue

De
Fontaine

La
Fontaine

Rochleaux
Road

Drilling-
court Rd

De Berange
Avenue

Fresnaye
Sports Club

**SEA
POINT**

Ocean

Bordeaux
Ave

View

Brank-
some Rd

Ave

Firdale
Ave

Deane Rd

Clifton Rd

Friars

Private

Barkley Rd

Level

Holmfirth

The Glen

Heathfield
Road

Firmount
Oldfield
Road

Dove Road

Kildare

Bakey
Road

Albany Rd

Lydgne

Rd

Regent Rd

3

Road

Hill

4

Table Mountain
National Park

Lion's Head
• 669m

5

Signal

6

126

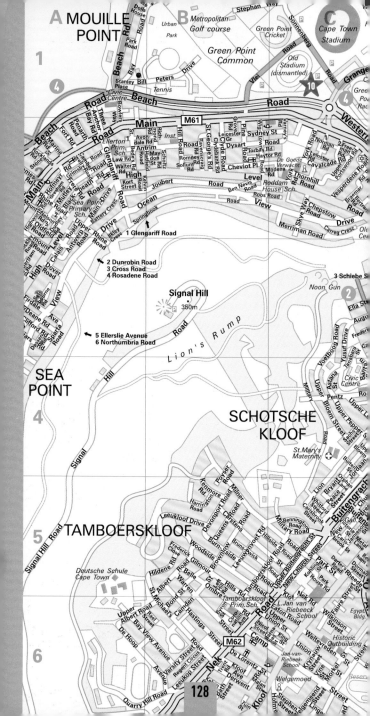

A MOUILLE POINT

B Metropolitan Golf course

Green Point Cricket

C Cape Town Stadium

Stephan Way

Sonnenberg

1

Urban Park

Dolls House

Park Road

Beach Road

Green Point Common

Old Stadium (dismantled)

Grange

Green Po

Western

Bay

Stanley Place

Bill

Peters

Tennis

Three Anchor Bay Rd

Civic Centre

Bowlers Way

10

Beach Road

Road

Road

M61

Main Road

Ellerton Rd

Avondale Rd

Antrim

St.George's Rd

Pine St

Sydney St

Varneys Rd

Norman Rd

2 Freeman Rd

2

Beach

Penarth Rd

Fort Rd

Marine

Road

Glengariff Rd

Law Rd

Walter Rd

Clydeann Rd

Road

Leicester Rd

Ravenscraig Rd

Cheviot Pl

Dysart Rd

Torbay Rd

De Goede Verwacht Modena

Cavalcade

Leinster Rd

Upper Portswood Rd

Vesperdene Road

Level

Thornhill

Road

Sollum Rd

Kelvin

Road

Ocean

Joubert

Road

Ben Nevis Road

Roddam House Sch.

Roos Road

View

Skye Way

Chepstow Road

Carreg Cresc

Drive

Battery Cresc

Springbok

Road

Merriman Road

1 Glengariff Road

Signal Hill

350m

Noon Gun

3 Schiebe S

2

Ella Str

Augu

2 Dunrobin Road
3 Cross Road
4 Rosadene Road

Lion's Rump

Road

5 Ellerslie Avenue
6 Northumbria Road

Voetboog Road

Yusuf Drive

Frieder

SEA POINT

Hill

Signal

Civic Centre

Pentz

Upper Bloem Street

Upper Pappe

Ro

4

Signal

SCHOTSCHE KLOOF

St.Mary's Maternity

Lion

Bryant

Orphan

Peace

Buitengrach

New

Whitford

Catastoop

St

Jordaan

5

Signal Hill Road

TAMBOERSKLOOF

Poyser Road

Kenmore

Milner

Road

Leeukloof Drive

Harrington Road

Bruns Road

Leeuwenvoet Rd

Hillside Rd

Bennington Road

Military Road

New Church Street

Park St

Rheede

Deutsche Schule Cape Town

Frederick Close

Hildene Road

Woodside Road

Burnlow side

Leeuwenvoet Rd

Gilmour

Belle

Tamboerskloof Prim.Sch.

Upper Buitengracht

Nek Rd

L.Jan van Riebeeck School

Kohling

House

Dixon Rd

Egypt Bldg.

6

Upper Albert Road

De Hoop

St Michael's

Camden

Warren

Bond St

Hastings

Hills Rd

Ombre

Road

Tamboerskloof Road

Upper Union St

Milton

Union St

Union

Welge

Wilkinson

Historic Outbuilding

Bay View Avenue

Rael St

Varsity Street

De Lorentz

M62

Camp

Nek Rd

Kloof Rd

Jan-van-Riebeeck School

Welgemoed

Stephen

Quarry Hill Road

Leeukloof Street

Derwent

Malan

Kloof

Holm

Reser

128

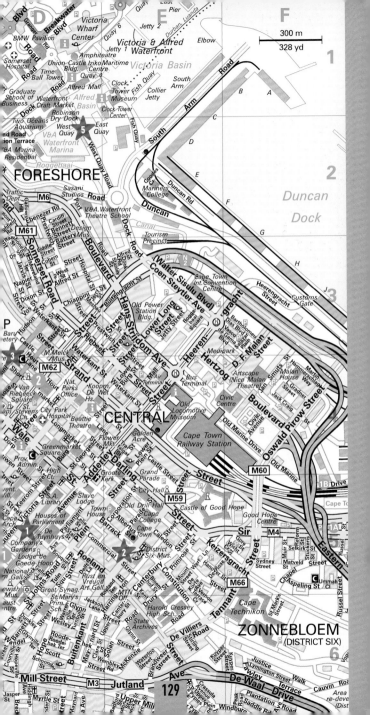

FORESHORE

CENTRAL

ZONNEBLOEM
(DISTRICT SIX)

Duncan Dock

Victoria Wharf Center
Victoria & Alfred Waterfront
Victoria Basin
Breakwater Blvd
BMW Pavilion
Somerset Hospital
Graduate School of Business
Amphitheatre
Union Castle Iziko Maritime Centre
Bldg.
Quay 4
Alfred Mall
Waterfront Craft Market
Dock Craft Market
Robinson Dry Dock
Two Oceans Aquarium
V&A Waterfront Marina
V&A Marina Residential
Roggebaai

Clock Tower Fish Quay
South Arm
Clock Tower Museum
Collier Jetty
Clock Tower Center
East Quay
West Quay

300 m
328 yd

Traffic Dept.
Sasani Studios Road
V&A Waterfront Theatre School
Design Bldg.
Old Power Station Bldg.
Canal
Tourism Precinct
Cape Town Int. Convention Centre
Heerengracht Street
Customs Gate
Mariners College
Duncan Rd

Cardiff Street
Bennett Street
Battery Mus.
Hans Strijdom Ave
Coen Steytler Ave
(Walter Sisulu Blvd)
Lower Long Street
Jetty Street
Bartholomew
Medipark
Artscape (Nico Malan) Theatres
Malan House Way
St Craig
St Greenmarket Square
M.Melck Mus.
Nat. Parks Office
Koopm. De Wet Hs.
Air Terminal
Bus Terminal
Civic Centre
Oswald Pirow Street
D.F. Malan Street
Hertzog Boulevard

City Park Hospital
Beattie Theatre
Old Locomotive Museum
Cape Town Railway Station
Old Marine Drive
Gardens Avenue

Greenmarket Square
Prov. Admin
Golden Acre
Flower Mkt.
Grand Parade
City Hall
Castle of Good Hope
Good Hope Centre
Cape Town Int. Convention

S.A. Library
Slave Lodge
Houses of Parliament
De Tuynhuys
Town House
Old Drill Hall
Cape Town College
District Six Mus.
Sydney Street
Matveld Street
Cummall

Company's Gardens
Lodge de Goede Hoop
National Gallery
Jewish Mus.
St Mary's Prim. Sch.
St Glynn
Rust en Vreugd Art Gall.
Cape Town MTN Off.
Harold Cressey High Sch.
State Archives
De Villiers Street
Cape Technikon
St Mark's Sch.
Justice Symington Street Walk

Mill Street
Jutland
De Waal Drive
Upper Mill
Cauvin Road
Windburg

129

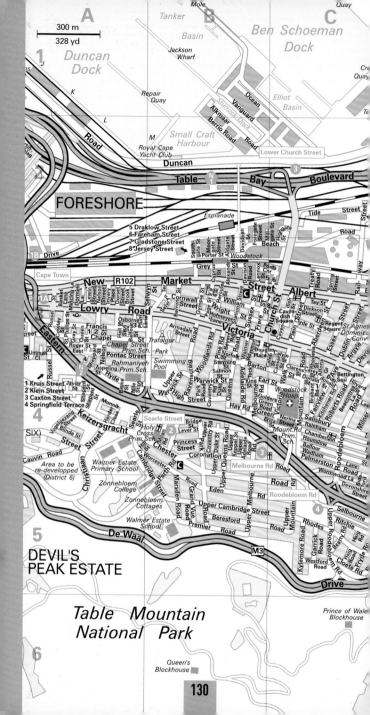

A

Mole

Tanker
Basin

Jackson
Wharf

300 m
328 yd

*Duncan
Dock*

1J

K

Repair
Quay

Royal Cape
Yacht Club

L

M

Duncan

Table

B

Quay

*Ben Schoeman
Dock*

Ocean
Vanguard

Alkmaar
Berrio Road

Small Craft
Harbour

Duncan

N

Bay

C

Cre
Quay

Elliot
Basin

Lower Church Street

Boulevard

FORESHORE

Esplanade

5 Draklow Street
6 Fareham Street
7 Gladstone Street
8 Jersey Street

Drive

Woodstock

Southgate St
Moorgate
Portergate Lane
Aldgate St
Davidson

Grey
St

Tide
Street

Road

Foregate St
Millgate St
Highgate St
Beach

Cape Town

**New
Lowry**

R102

Market

Street

Albert

Road

Road

Lewin St
Nelson St
Inway Place
Invard Street
Dorset St
Brook St

Selwyn

St

Cornwall
Street

William

Gympie St
Page St
Wright
Holmeyer
Lane

Church St

Cavendish Square

Tay St
Dickson St
Hyde St

St Regent
Square

Spring St

Treaty Road

Essex St

Dublin St

Dominica
Conv

Basket Lane
Mincing La
Dromhill
Lane

Russel

Gowly St
Grey St
Roger St East

Francis
Chapel St

Pontac Street

Osborne St
Hall St
Chapel Street

Trafalgar
Park

Armadale
Street

Victoria

Pine Rd
Brydon Rd
Hercules
Walmer

Clarence St
Wall St
Calvin
Douglas
Place

St Phillips St
Roger St

Rahmaniyeh
Prim. Sch.

Aspeling St

Hyde St

Swimming
Pool

Woodlands Rd
Barton
Stevning

Salmon
St

Clarens St

St Donald St

Golders
Green Rd

Plein
St

Chr
Cavendish St

Spring St

Brabant
Richmond Rd
Roberts Rd
Fairview
Golders

Bettington
Squ

Hilkard
Rd

Beacons

1 Kruis Street
2 Klein Street
3 Caxton Street
4 Springfield Terrace

Javier St
Russel

Bedce
St
Lyle St

St

Upper

Warwick

High
Street

Adelaide Rd
Queens

King Earl St
Green

Hay Rd

Nerina
Street

Woodstock
Hosp.

Mount.Rd

Mountain

Salisbury
Rainham

Chamberlain

Devonshire
Street

SIX)

Voogelzang

Blinde St

Keizersgracht

Munnik

Searle
Cross Lane

Searle Street

Holy
Cross
Prim. Sch.

Bridge St
Lever St

Princess
Street

Coventry Rd
Duke St
Keppel St
Upper
Norfolk

Melbourne Rd

Hounslow
Balfour
Wadham
Palmerston

Road

Road

Street

Road

**Area to be
re-developed
(District 6)**

Cauvin Road

Walmer Estate
Primary School

Zonnebloem
College

Zonnebloem
Cottages

Walmer Estate
School

De Waal

Chester

Cambridge
Street

Marsden Road

Coronation

Upper Queens Road

Worcester

Road

Eden

Grand Vue
Road

Upper Cambridge Street

Beresford

Premier
Road

Melbourne
Rd

Roodebloem Rd

Upper
Mountain
Road

Mount.
Prim.
Sch.

Rd

Rhodes

Road

Wormwood La
Roodebloem

Lane
Rd

Selbourne
Ritchie

Garrick Road
Westford
Road

Cloete Rd

Upper Roodebloem Road

Kylemore Road

M3

**DEVIL'S
PEAK ESTATE**

Drive

*Table   Mountain
National   Park*

Prince of Wale
Blockhouse

5

6

Queen's
Blockhouse

130

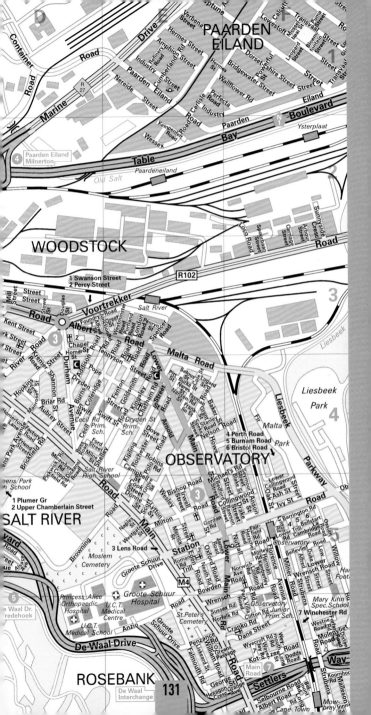

PAARDEN EILAND

WOODSTOCK

OBSERVATORY

SALT RIVER

ROSEBANK

1 Swanson Street
2 Percy Street

4 Perth Road
5 Burnam Road
6 Bristol Road

1 Plumer Gr
2 Upper Chamberlain Street

3 Lens Road

7 Winchester Rd

Marine Road
Container Road
Table Bay Boulevard
Eiland Boulevard
Paarden Bay
Old Salt
Paardeneiland
Voortrekker Road
Albert Road
Malta Road
Lower Road
Main Road
Durham Avenue
Liesbeek Parkway
Liesbeek Park
Groote Schuur Drive
De-Waal-Drive
Settlers Way

Groote Schuur Hospital
Princess Alice Orthopaedic Hospital
U.C.T. Medical Centre
U.C.T. Medical School
Moslem Cemetery
St. Peter's Cemetery
Salt River Prim. Sch.
Salt River High School
Observatory Junior Prim. Sch.
Mary Kihn Spec. School

R102
R27
M4

De Waal Interchange
De Waal Dr. Oranjezicht

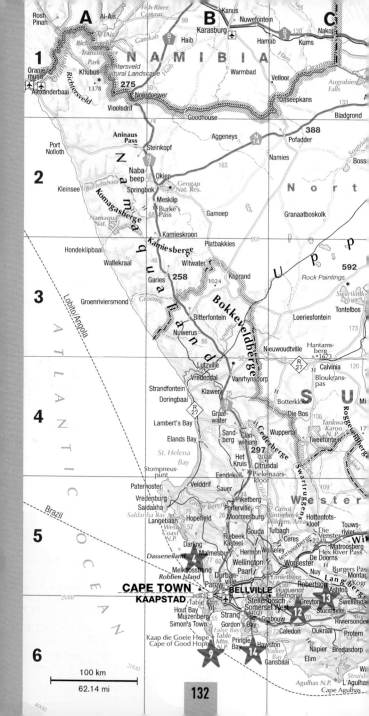

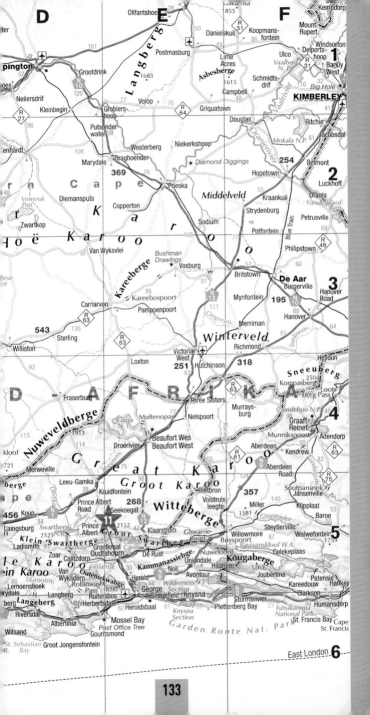

This index lists a selection of the streets and squares shown in the street atlas

KEY TO STREET ATLAS

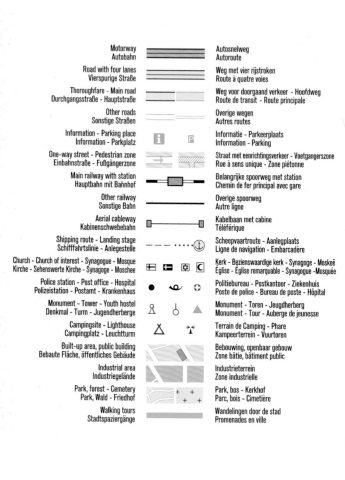

English / German		English / Dutch / French
Motorway / Autobahn		Autosnelweg / Autoroute
Road with four lanes / Vierspurige Straße		Weg met vier rijstroken / Route à quatre voies
Thoroughfare - Main road / Durchgangsstraße - Hauptstraße		Weg voor doorgaand verkeer - Hoofdweg / Route de transit - Route principale
Other roads / Sonstige Straßen		Overige wegen / Autres routes
Information - Parking place / Information - Parkplatz		Informatie - Parkeerplaats / Information - Parking
One-way street - Pedestrian zone / Einbahnstraße - Fußgängerzone		Straat met eenrichtingverkeer - Voetgangerszone / Rue à sens unique - Zone piétonne
Main railway with station / Hauptbahn mit Bahnhof		Belangrijke spoorweg met station / Chemin de fer principal avec gare
Other railway / Sonstige Bahn		Overige spoorweg / Autre ligne
Aerial cableway / Kabinenschwebebahn		Kabelbaan met cabine / Téléférique
Shipping route - Landing stage / Schifffahrtslinie - Anlegestelle		Scheepvaartroute - Aanlegplaats / Ligne de navigation - Embarcadère
Church - Church of interest - Synagogue - Mosque / Kirche - Sehenswerte Kirche - Synagoge - Moschee		Kerk - Bezienswaardige kerk - Synagoge - Moskeë / Église - Église remarquable - Synagogue -Mosquée
Police station - Post office - Hospital / Polizeistation - Postamt - Krankenhaus		Politiebureau - Postkantoor - Ziekenhuis / Poste de police - Bureau de poste - Hôpital
Monument - Tower - Youth hostel / Denkmal - Turm - Jugendherberge		Monument - Toren - Jeugdherberg / Monument - Tour - Auberge de jeunesse
Campingsite - Lighthouse / Campingplatz - Leuchtturm		Terrain de Camping - Phare / Kampeerterrein - Vuurtoren
Built-up area, public building / Bebaute Fläche, öffentliches Gebäude		Bebouwing, openbaar gebouw / Zone bâtie, bâtiment public
Industrial area / Industriegelände		Industrieterrein / Zone industrielle
Park, forest - Cemetery / Park, Wald - Friedhof		Park, bos - Kerkhof / Parc, bois - Cimetière
Walking tours / Stadtspaziergänge		Wandelingen door de stad / Promenades en ville

INDEX

This index lists all sights, museums, estates and destinations as well as important places, streets, persons and keywords in this guide. Numbers in bold indicate a main entry.

WRITE TO US

e-mail: info@marcopologuides.co.uk

Did you have a great holiday?
Is there something on your mind?
Whatever it is, let us know!
Whether you want to praise, alert us
to errors or give us a personal tip –
MARCO POLO would be pleased to
hear from you.
We do everything we can to provide the
very latest information for your trip.

Nevertheless, despite all of our authors'
thorough research, errors can creep in.
MARCO POLO does not accept any
liability for this. Please contact us by
e-mail or post.

MARCO POLO Travel Publishing Ltd
Pinewood, Chineham Business Park
Crockford Lane, Chineham
Basingstoke, Hampshire RG24 8AL
United Kingdom

PICTURE CREDITS
Cover photograph: False Bay's brightly coloured changing cabins (Getty Images/Taxi: Gavin Hellier)
Die Afrikaanse Taalmuseum: Melinda Bonthuys (16 centre); C. Bäck (18/19); W. Dieterich (front flap left, front flap
right, 3 centre, 20, 30, 32, 34, 36, 38, 40, 44, 47, 56, 61, 63, 71, 72/73, 74, 79, 82, 86, 96/97, 98, 101, 102, 109, 110, 112,
116 top, 116 bottom); DuMont Bildarchiv: Selbach (94, 95, 106, 112/113); J. Frangenberg (2 centre bottom, 26/27, 49,
52/53, 104/105, 113); F. M. Frei (3 bottom, 8, 80/81, 94/95); Getty Images: Dominic Barnardt (1 bottom); Getty Images/
Taxi: Gavin Hellier (1 top); Huber: Gräfenhain (2 centre top, 7, 10/11, 15, 25, 43, 51, 137), Ripani (24 right); Ilan (17 top);
© iStockphoto.com: Sasa Radovic (16 top); Laif: Emmler (69, 117); Look: Coelfen (62 left); E. Losskarn (59); mauritius
images: Africa Media Online (22/23), Alamy (2 top, 3 top, 4, 5, 6, 12/13, 24 right, 62 right, 64/65, 66, 76, 88/89,
90, 92), CuboImages (85), cultura (9); mauritius images/imagebroker/White Star/Ryogo i Kubo (2 bottom, 54/55);
Christian Putsch (1 bottom); T. Stankiewicz (128/129); The Test Kitchen (17 bottom); Volunturs (16 bottom)

1st Edition 2013
Worldwide Distribution: Marco Polo Travel Publishing Ltd, Pinewood, Chineham Business Park,
Crockford Lane, Basingstoke, Hampshire RG24 8AL, United Kingdom. Email: sales@marcopolouk.com
© MAIRDUMONT GmbH & Co. KG, Ostfildern
Chief editors: Michaela Lienemann (concept, managing editor), Marion Zorn (concept, text editor)
Authors: Anja Jeschonneck, Kai Schächtele; co-autor: Christian Putsch; editor: Jochen Schürmann
Programme supervision: Ann-Katrin Kutzner, Nikolai Michaelis
Picture editor: Gabriele Forst
What's hot: wunder media, Munich
Cartography street atlas: © MAIRDUMONT, Ostfildern; Cartography pull-out map: © MAIRDUMONT, Ostfildern
Design: milchhof : atelier, Berlin; Front cover, pull-out map cover, page 1: factor product munich
Translated from German by Birgitt Lederer; editor of the English edition: Margaret Howie, fullproof.co.za
Prepress: M. Feuerstein, Wigel

DOS & DON'TS ☝

A few things you should bear in mind when in Cape Town

DO NOT GIVE MONEY TO CHILD BEGGARS

Cape Town's traffic intersections can turn into a hive of activity as soon as the light turns red. Newspaper vendors, street vendors (selling anything from cheap sunglasses to wire toys) and sadly also child beggars. Even if hard to do so, it is best not to give them money. Cape Town's social workers are working hard at getting the situation under control because the children either use the money for drugs or have to hand it over to their syndicate bosses.

DO NOT GO UP THE MOUNTAINS AT NIGHT

As inviting as a view of Cape Town by night from above may seem, it is advisable not to take your car up Signal Hill or attempt a solo climb up Lion's Head at night. You may fall prey to thieves who take advantage of the isolation of the mountains. There are nevertheless still many safe ways to see the city's flickering lights from above. Join an organised full moon hike up Lion's Head and whatever you do always keep in mind the age-old adage: safety in numbers.

DO PLAN YOUR HIKE UP TABLE MOUNTAIN

Capetonians can only look on in disbelief at how some tourists approach the hike up Table Mountain. They set off equipped with no more than a camera and a tube of suntan lotion. More often than not they realise their mistake too late when suddenly they find themselves enveloped in a thick fog or rain clouds near the plateau. It is essential not to underestimate the mountain and to prepare for your hike properly beforehand! Check the weather forecast, make sure you have the right gear and provisions (see 'Sightseeing') and never attempt the climb alone. If you come properly prepared, the magnificent views from the top, after what can at times be quite a strenuous climb, will be your much deserved reward.

DO AVOID THE PEAK TRAFFIC

Rush hour traffic on the motorways heading into Cape Town city centre can be very bad on weekdays between 6.30am and 8.30am. You are bound to be stuck in traffic jams and the same goes for the end of the working day with the same scenario unfolding again in the opposite direction. Best to avoid driving in peak hours altogether!

DO LOOK AFTER YOUR VALUABLES

Be it wallet, camera, jewellery or items of clothing, do look after your valuables and don't leave anything in your car that may attract attention. You don't want to come back to a car that has been broken into with all your possessions gone. The car boot is no safe place for valuables either. The cardinal rule is to take with you only what you can carry.